上海市教委“085工程”地方本科高校内涵建设项目·
外国语言学及应用语言学重点学科建设项目(Z085YY JJ13001)

英语冠词系统习得中的标记理论和语言迁移研究

A Study on Markedness and Language Transfer in the Acquisition of the English Article System

赵海艳 著

山东大学出版社

图书在版编目(CIP)数据

英语冠词系统习得中的标记理论和语言迁移研究/赵海艳著.
—济南:山东大学出版社,2014.6
ISBN 978-7-5607-5130-6

Ⅰ.①英…　Ⅱ.①赵…　Ⅲ.①英语—冠词—语言学习—研究
Ⅳ.①H313

中国版本图书馆 CIP 数据核字(2014)第 207951 号

责任策划:陈海军
责任编辑:王　潇　郑琳琳
封面设计:张　荔

出版发行:山东大学出版社
社　址　山东省济南市山大南路 20 号
邮　编　250100
电　话　市场部(0531)88364466
经　销:山东省新华书店
印　刷:济南景升印业有限公司
规　格:850 毫米×1160 毫米　1/32
8.125 印张　204 千字
版　次:2014 年 6 月第 1 版
印　次:2014 年 6 月第 1 次印刷
定　价:30.00 元

前　言

本书是根据我的博士论文《英语冠词系统习得中的标记理论和语言迁移研究》修改而成的，全书共分为 7 章。本研究以二语习得理论中的母语迁移理论和标记理论为基础，运用定量研究和定性研究相结合的方法，对不同母语背景下的语言学习者在英语冠词系统习得过程中标记性差异与母语迁移产生的关系，即母语迁移何时产生以及如何产生的情况进行了探索性研究。

在理论上，本研究从一个全新的角度，即在标记理论的框架下对英语冠词系统习得过程中的母语迁移现象进行了分析。英语冠词作为限定词的一种，与名词或名词词组连用，在语言交际中使用频率较高，对语言交际能否成功起着一定的限定作用。因此英语冠词系统习得是二语学习者英语语言习得中的重要组成部分。冠词主要存在于印欧语系及闪语当中，而汉语属于汉藏语系，并没有冠词系统，因此不同母语背景下的语言学习者可能会由于母语迁移的作用，对冠词的习得出现差异。对于冠词系统的研究，在国外著述颇多，包括冠词系统的分类、指称意义、冠词的习得顺序以及学习者第二语言对冠词系统习得的影响等。在国内，近年来对英语冠词的研究主要分为三类：对英语冠词语义功能的研究、英语冠词的教学研究和英语冠词的习得研究。对于冠词的研究，前人多注重于学习者母语与目的语之间句法和语义的比较研究，而这种研究多建立在对比分析的基础之上，而对比分析无法解释为何母语与目的语之间的差异并不总是产生习得困难的现象。因此，本研究从标记理论的角度对英语冠词系统习得中的母语迁移现象进行研究，试图探索英语冠词习得过程中标记性差异与母语可迁移性的关系。本研究将以国外二语习得环境中不同母语背景下的语言学习者作为研究对象，就二语学习者在相同的语言环境下由于母语体系中是否存在冠词系统的差异，对英语冠词系统的习得所产生的影响进行研究，并从标记理论和语言迁移的角度出发，就可能存在的差异进行分析，以期能够找到英语冠词习得中标记理论与母语迁移所产生的作用，并找出相应的解决办法。

在研究方法上，本研究运用了定量研究和定性研究相结合的方法。通过对试题成绩的统计分析、冠词频数的语料库分析以及试后回访等定量与定性研究相结合的方法，从标记理论的视角，就不同母语背景下的语言学习者在冠词习得过程中所存在的母语迁移现象进行分析，将思辨性、理论性研究与实证性研究方法相结合，从而进行多层次的横向对比研究。首先，本研究采用实验研究的方法，通过单项选择和短文填空对语言学习者冠词的习得情况以及其他限定词与冠词成绩的对比进行分析。按照 Huebner 对冠词以二项对立特征，即名词词组语义环境特指（specific reference）和听者知识（assumed known/not known to the hearer）为参照的分类方法将冠词分为四类：定指，类指，不定指，无指。实验运用 SPSS 统计软件，对相同母语背景下的语言学习者在不同的冠词词类中的成绩是否存在差异以及不同母语背景下的语言学习者对于相同的冠词词类的掌握是否存在差异进行定量分析。其次，其他限定词在名词短语中起到了与冠词相似的对名词的限定作用，从而加大了冠词习得的复杂性。因此，本项研究将其他限定词的研究也包含在内，主要研究了冠词的使用与其他限定词的掌握是否存在差异；语言学习者为了避免错误的产生，在习得冠词的过程中是否存在避免使用冠词而缺省冠词的现象，或由于学习者知晓冠词使用频率较高而存在过度使用的现象。此外，本研究还通过试后回访了解学生选择不同冠词或其他限定词的原因，从而进一步了解不同母语背景下的语言学习者对冠词的掌握情况，对冠词系统习得中标记理论和母语迁移产生的心理因素进行定性分析。试后回访通过对学习者提供答案的内在心理原因进行划分，探知标记理论视角下母语迁移的心理认知是随意发生的，还是选择性的、系统性的。这种定量研究和定性研究相结合的研究方法使研究者得以更好地掌握和分析不同母语背景下语言学习者对英语冠词的习得情况。

在研究对象上，本研究中的实验对象选取了不同母语背景下的语言学习者。国外对于冠词系统的研究较多，但鲜有把中国学生作为研究对象的研究；相反，国内的研究多以国内外语环境下的语言学习者作为研究对象，研究汉语对英语冠词习得的影响。本论文中的实验对象为来自英国中兰卡郡大学的 43 名非英语专业本科生，包括母语中包含冠词系统的西班牙语和法语的学生以及母语中缺乏冠词系统的汉语的学生。本研究通过对国外二语习得环境下母语中有无冠词系统的语言学习者对英语冠词习得的差异情况进行分析，进而探索在标记理论框架下英语冠词习得过程中的母语迁移现象，对于进一步了解母语迁移的可行性，以及如何促进母语的正迁移、减少母语的负迁移具有一定的研究意义和参考价值。

本研究对今后二语习得研究中通过标记理论和母语迁移理论分析英语冠词系统的实证研究以及国内英语冠词系统的教学研究具有一定的参考意义。例如，对不同英语冠词指称类别掌握的差异进行的研究，对于教师在指导学生类指、回指等不同类别的学习中采用不同的教学方法，从而有效地提高学生对冠词的掌握具有一定的促进作用；通过促进教师在教学中对英语冠词系统标记性差异进行对比，尽量减少母语负迁移等等。

本书在出版过程中得到了“上海市教委‘085 工程’地方本科

高校内涵建设项目·外国语言学及应用语言学重点学科建设项目”的资助，并得到了山东大学出版社的大力支持，在此一并表示衷心的感谢！

赵海艳

2014 年 4 月

List of Abbreviations

ACP	Article Choice Parameter
ANOVA	Analysis of Variance
BPH	Biological Program Hypothesis
CAH	Contrastive Analysis Hypothesis
CC	Creative Construction
CR	Contrastive Rhetoric
CUP	Common Underlying Proficiency
DP	Determiner Phrase
EFL	English as a foreign language
ESK	Explicitly Stated Knowledge
ESL	English as a second language
FA	Full Access Hypothesis
FH	Fluctuation Hypothesis
FT	Full Transfer Hypothesis
HK	Hearer's Knowledge
MDH	Markedness Differential Hypothesis
MSIH	Missing Surface Inflection Hypothesis
MTH	Minimal Trees Hypothesis
NCEE	National College Entrance Examination
NL	Native Language
NMP	Nominal Mapping Parameter

NP	Noun Phrase
RDH	Representational Deficit Hypothesis
SLA	Second Language Acquisition
SPSS	Statistical Package for the Social Sciences
SR	Specific Referent
TL	Target Language
UG	Universal Grammar

List of Tables

List of Figures

Contents

Chapter 1 Introduction

1.1 Goals

This book aims to explore the L2 acquisition of the English article system from the perspective of markedness and language transfer in the hope of contributing to the research of second language acquisition and foreign language teaching.

Articles are functional words and play an important part in second language research. There is a lot of evidence that articles are among the most commonly used words in English (Butler, 2002). *A*, *an*, and *the*, along with the zero article (∅), account for 8.5% in the whole English discourse (Berry, 1993). Therefore, it is of great significance for the second language learners to master the usage of articles. What's more, it is difficult to manipulate the English article system due to the complex semantic classification and specific usages of the English articles. Just as Master (1990: 461) claimed, "the English article system is one of the most difficult aspects of English grammar for nonnative speakers and one of the latest to be fully acquired". Master (2002) summarizes three main difficulties language learners encounter in the process of article acquisition. Firstly, the high frequency of articles presented both in speech and text description makes it difficult to identify a rule from too many usages. Secondly, function words are not usually taken for emphasis, which makes them harder to notice. And thirdly, the article system has only one morpheme for many different uses in English. This one-to-many mapping contributes to the complexity of the article acquisition. Therefore, the complexity of articles poses a great challenge to English language learners, especially to those whose native languages, like Chinese, do not have article system.

Many languages which contain articles belong to the Indo-European language family, whereas Chinese belongs to the Sino-Tibetan family which is acknowledged as a language without article system. In other words, there are no functional equivalents in Chinese of the English article system. "Definiteness and specificity are marked in Chinese by word order or the use of determiners." (Robertson, 2000: 140) For Chinese learners, English articles are a category of zero contrast (Zobl, 1982). Therefore, Chinese language learners may, due to the typological difference and the role of language transfer, frequently make errors in the process of acquiring the article system. Ample evidence shows that Chinese learners find it particularly difficult to acquire English articles.

High frequency of articles in discourses and the difficulty of fully acquiring them have aroused researchers' interest. They have investigated the articles from many aspects: the classification of the article system (Christopherson, 1939;

Hawkins, 1978; Bickerton, 1981; Huebner, 1983; Chesterman, 1991; Lyons, 1999; Krifka, 1995), the acquisition order of the articles (Huebner, 1983; Parrish, 1987; Liu and Gleason, 2002), reference of articles and the impact of native language on the acquisition of article system (Larsen-Freeman, 1976; Ringbom, 1985; Young, 1996; Robertson, 2000). Domestic studies of English articles mainly focus on the complex specific usages of each type of article. Only in the past two decades did researchers begin to study English articles. The studies so far can be roughly divided into three categories: literature review of English article acquisition (Yang, 2009; Zhou, 2008), the study of teaching of English articles and the sequence of acquisition of English articles (Yan, 2003; Wang, 2005; Li and Yang, 2010), and the relationship between the article acquisition and language proficiency (Dai and Wei, 2008; Wei and Dai, 2010; Zhu, 2003; Li and Yang, 2010).

The book explores the functions of markedness and language transfer in article acquisition. The subjects of the tests were language learners with different native languages: English, Spanish, French and Chinese respectively. The study attempts to apply quantitative and qualitative research method to analyze the difference between language learners with different native languages concerning article acquisition. It will further analyze the psychological factors to explore the underlying features of language transfer and markedness in the process of article acquisition. It is hoped that the present study will bring some implications to SLA study and foreign language teaching.

1.2 Research Questions

The present study aims to address the following three questions:

(1) When do language transfer and markedness happen in the process of article acquisition?

(2) How do language transfer and markedness function in the process of article acquisition?

(3) Psychologically, is language transfer systematic or at random?

This book consists of two experiments. The two experiments are conducted to investigate when and how language transfer and markedness function in the process of article acquisition. 43 international students with different native languages were required to finish a multiple-choice task and a blank-filling task. Statistical analyses include the differences between the [+ART] group and the [−ART] group and the differences between four semantic types of articles. The third question is addressed by a series of semi-structured interviews. The participants were required to state the reasons to make their choices. Through the analyses of specific and non-specific reasons, the author explores the psychological effect of language transfer and markedness.

1.3 Significance of the Study

The significance and originality of the present study lie in the following aspects. First, the present study investigates the article acquisition from a new perspective: language transfer and markedness. The previous studies usually focus on the syntactic or semantic comparison between the target language and the learners' native language. The syntactic or semantic comparison based on Contrastive Analysis Hypothesis (CAH) claims that all the learning difficulties can be attributed to the differences between the target language and the learner's native language. However, it can not explain why some differences between target language and the learners' native languages will not lead to the learning difficulties among language learners. Therefore, the author attempts to explore the article acquisition from the perspective of markedness and language transfer in the hope of probing into the possibility of language transfer and the learning difficulty through analyzing the degree of markedness.

Second, a psychological analysis of markedness and language transfer in article acquisition is employed in this study. The examination of the comparison of the markedness between the learners' native languages and target language lacks the access to the internal reasons for the occurrence of language transfer. It is of great significance to investigate how language learners perceive markedness and when language transfer happens. The present study employs a series of semi-structured interviews to examine the perception of the learners when they are making the choice to have a better understanding of the process of article acquisition.

Third, the participants of the study involve learners with different native backgrounds, with a particular focus on Chinese learners. The researches abroad are extensive, but very few of them have taken Chinese learners as subjects (Robertson, 2000; Wong, 2007). On the other hand, the subjects in domestic studies are mainly Chinese college students and the materials are mostly from the Chinese Learner English Corpus (CLEC). Few studies have compared Chinese learners with the learners whose native languages have an article system. The current study includes both Chinese learners and learners with different native backgrounds with view of making a comprehensive comparison between [+ART] group and [−ART] group.

To sum up, the current study in this book is significant in three ways: investigation of the article acquisition from language transfer and markedness, the application of psychological analysis of the article acquisition and involvement of both Chinese learners and foreign language learners.

1.4 Framework

This book consists of seven chapters. The present chapter mainly explains the goals, the research questions, the significance of the study and the framework of this book.

Chapter 2 reviews the previous studies in the past several

decades concerning language transfer and markedness to lay a theoretical and experimental foundation for the present study. It introduces various definitions of language transfer and markedness, controversial views on the functions of language transfer as well as different criteria for markedness.

Chapter 3 presents the previous experimental studies of article acquisition in SLA. Due to the significance and complexity of the article system, the SLA studies investigate the article system from many different aspects. The author summarizes the theoretical and experimental studies of article acquisition from two perspectives: linguistic perspective and psychological perspective. Meanwhile, some limitations of the previous studies and the creative part of the present study are also pointed out.

Chapter 4 and Chapter 5 report the experiments conducted in the study and form the main body of the book together with Chapter 6. Chapter 4 reports the experiment which focuses on the differences between the [+ART] group and [−ART] group L2 learners as well as the acquisition differences among four semantic article types. Three research questions are answered: the differences of mean scores between the [+ART] group and [−ART] group L2 learners, the acquisition differences among four semantic article types as well as whether language transfer will happen in article acquisition due to different degree of markedness among [+ART] group L2 learners and [−ART] group L2 learners. Research method is described in detail. The experimental results based on the statistical analysis are discussed and analyzed.

Chapter 5 reports the study of articles and other

determiners, including the qualitative and quantitative analyses of articles and other determiners. Three questions are raised: correct and incorrect frequency and percentage of articles and other determiners among the students with different native languages, the possible overuse or underuse in the usage of articles and the correct frequency of the four semantic types of articles. In this Experiment, a blank-filling task is designed, and the same participants in Experiment 1 participated in the second experiment right after finishing the first one.

Chapter 6 is a series of qualitative semi-structured interviews, conducted to investigate the psychological reasons behind the subjects' choice of articles. It aims to gather further information to support the quantitative research and to shed light on the second language learners' metalinguistic knowledge in their use of articles.

Chapter 7 summarizes the major findings and discusses some theoretical and pedagogical implications. It also points out the limitations of the study and the directions for future studies on this topic.

Chapter 2 Language Transfer and Markedness Theory

Before I delve into the study of article acquisition, a review of language transfer and markedness is needed. This chapter first reviews the previous theoretical and experimental studies on language transfer and markedness in second language acquisition (SLA). It gives a general overview of the definition of language transfer and three different views on language transfer are introduced in detail. Following that are the definition, criteria, as well as the theoretical and experimental studies of markedness.

2.1 Language Transfer in SLA

Language transfer, or cross-linguistic influence, has been a crucial theoretical construct in applied linguistics, SLA and language teaching (Odlin, 1989). The concept of transfer is borrowed from psychology. It refers to the sort of learning activities in which the outcome of learners' later learning or training behavior is influenced by their previously acquired knowledge (Croft, 1990). Over the past several decades, many studies have been carried out from different perspectives of transfer, such as the transfer of rhetorical redundancy (Bartlet, 1980, 1983; Al-Jarrah, 2001), pragmatic transfer (Hackmann, 1977; Kasper, 1979a, 1979b, 1992; Leech, 1983; Yuh-Fang, 2009), and the transfer of textual organization (Fakhri, 1994; Anthony, 2010). However, language transfer is still such a controversial concept that different scholars hold widely different views on it. It is not easy to single out a unitary concept which is completely exact and accurate. This section first reviews some representative views on the notion of language transfer in SLA.

Lado (1957) proposes Contrastive Analysis Hypothesis (CAH) and holds that second language learners rely almost entirely on their native language in the process of learning the target language. Based on behaviorist theory, CAH claims that the major impediment to learning is interference from prior knowledge (Ellis, 1999). Dulay and Burt (1974a, 1974b) put forward the hypothesis of Creative Construction (CC) and argue that in the process of acquiring a target language, the native language plays no role, namely, non-transfer. Chomsky initiates in the mid-1960s restructuring the concept of Universal Grammar (UG) and argues that UG is a theory of innate principles, the starting point of language acquisition. According to UG, human beings can produce a language with a deep structure which enables them to generate language grammar which can be transferred to any other language. UG is considered to be a human-specific language acquisition device. However, Corder (1981) questions the definition. He prefers to use the notion of "role of mother tongue", rather than language transfer. He further classifies the influence of native language into two types: borrowing and structural transfer. Corder insists that the learner's native language does produce some effect on second language learning, but it is only the urgent "borrowing" when the learners' knowledge of the target language is not sufficient. Selinker (1972) puts forth the concept "interlanguage" which refers to the systematic knowledge of language independent of both the learner's native language and the target language. Nemser (1971) calls it *approximative systems*, and Corder (1971) calls it *idiosyncratic dialects* and *transitional competence*. It is a systematic continuum between the learner's native language and the target language. Selinker (1972) claims that interlanguage includes five central factors: language transfer, overgeneralization of L2 rules, transfer of training, strategies of L2 learning and communication strategies. According to interlanguage theory, language transfer is not interference but a cognitive process. Selinker notes that the features of the learner's native language are not transferred to the target language but the interlanguage. Language learners preserve some features of their native language or overgeneralize target language rules, and then approximate the target language.

Attempting to clarify the misunderstanding of language transfer, Odlin (2001) has conducted a series of studies in the past decade and points out the inappropriate aspects of the previous observations about transfer, and gives a comparatively briefer and more precise definition:

> Transfer is the influence resulting from similarities and differences

> between the target language and any other language that has been previously (and perhaps imperfectly) acquired.
>
> (Odlin, 2001: 27)

This definition offers a generally comprehensive and original account of the nature of language transfer and explains the essential role of native language in SLA. It is widely accepted that language transfer occurs in SLA and it is seen to interact with a number of other factors.

Controversial views on the notion of language transfer lead to different and even opposite views on manifestations of transfer. Traditionally, the manifestations of language transfer can be divided into three representative views: negative transfer that interferes with successful acquisition, zero transfer that completely denies the existence of transfer, and positive transfer that facilitates SLA. Three different types of manifestation of language transfer will be introduced next.

2.1.1 Manifestations of Transfer

Traditionally, the studies of language transfer can be classified into three types based on the influence of native language: negative transfer, zero transfer and positive transfer. The first type supports the negative influence of native language, namely, negative transfer. The representative theories are CAH (Lado, 1957) and Contrastive Rhetoric (CR) (Kaplan, 2001). CAH assumes that the differences between the native language and the target language lead to interference, thus resulting in errors in second language learning. Errors and difficulties in learning can be predicted through the comparison of the similarities and differences between the native language and the target language. CR claims that the cultural conventions and knowledge in the first language negatively influence the way L2 writers organize the written discourse in the second language. The main concern of CR is to help L2 learners overcome L1 interference in their L2 writing.

The second type claims that L2 learning has its own intrinsic order and sequence and is not affected by L1. The representative theories are the minimalist position and the Creative Construction hypothesis (CC) (Dulay and Burt, 1974a, 1974b) which emphasizes the innate mental mechanisms that L2 learners universally employ, and argues that L2 learning is largely unaffected by L1 transfer. The role of the learners' first language in L2 learning is minimal.

The third type argues that L1 facilitates L2 learning. The representative views are the hypothesis of Common Underlying Proficiency (CUP), the Full Access/Full Transfer Hypothesis (FA/FT) and Minimal Trees Hypothesis (MTH). These views arguc that an underlying proficiency exists in all languages and L1 facilitates rather than hinders L2 learning. These three types of language transfer will be explained in detail one by one in the following part.

2.1.1.1 Negative Transfer

Lado and Fries are the names most closely associated with CAH. CAH is based on the theory of behaviorism. The basic concept of CAH is that the structure of one language can be used in direct comparison with that of another one. Through the process of 'mapping' one structure onto another, the similarities and differences can be identified. According to CAH, identifying the differences results in a better understanding of the potential problems L2 learners will face. Different structural areas between the two languages will lead to interference, which is viewed as the transfer of elements of one language to another at various levels such as phonological, lexical and grammatical levels. Weinreich (1953) defines interference as those instances of deviation from the norms of either language which occur in the speech of bilinguals as a result of their familiarity with more than one language. Dakin (1973) identifies three principles based on CAH. The first is the principle of exercise which deems that language learners can promote their learning through making active and repeated responses to stimuli. The second is the principle of effect which emphasizes the significance of reinforcing the learners' response by rewarding correct response. The third is the principle of shaping which claims that language learning can be successful when complex behavior is separated into segments and learnt again and again. "Underlying these principles was the assumption that language learning, like any other kind of learning, took the form of habit formation, a habit consisting of an automatic response elicited by a given stimulus." (cited in Rod Ellis, 1999: 299) The central notion of CAH is that difference equates difficulty. In a specific attempt to rationalize language teaching materials, Fries (1945) writes:

> The most effective materials are those that are based upon a scientific description of the language to be learned, carefully compared with a parallel description of the native language of the learner.
>
> (Fries, 1945: 56)

CAH is based on a rigorous step-by-step comparison between the native language and the target language. This comparison covers every aspect of language such as phonology, morphology, syntax, and culture. The basic assumption of CAH is that the learners tend to transfer every aspect, such as the forms, meanings, culture and the distribution of their native language to the target language. Fries argues that the key to degrees of difficulty lies in the comparison between the native language and the target language.

Based on behaviorist theory, CAH proponents emphasize two important viewpoints: Firstly, transfer from the native language to the target language happens definitely in the process of L2 learning, and usually it is negative transfer. In other words, differences make difficulties. Secondly, learning difficulties can be predicted by comparing the linguistic differences between the two languages. The degree of difficulty depends largely on to what extent the L2 patterns are similar to or different from L1 patterns. If two structures are identical, learning will take place easily; otherwise, learning difficulties will arise and errors will occur due to the negative transfer caused by the differences.

CAH had its heyday in the 1960s, but fell out of favor in the 1970s. Its claims about the predictive power of the differences between the native and the target language were questioned in the 1970s. Some scholars (White, 1986; Rivers, 1970) claim that the comparison is only effective for explaining why certain errors arise, but not for predicting the errors in the absence of actual data about learners' errors. Other researchers, however, try to offer the empirical argument for the predictive power of CAH. To what extent can CAH predict the difficulties that language learners encounter has hitherto remained a controversial topic. To rationalize CAH, Wardhaugh (1970) proposes two versions of CAH: the Strong Version and the Weak Version. The former claims that CAH can predict the difficulties language learners may encounter while the latter argues that CAH can only explain the difficulties rather than predict them. Wardhaugh holds that the Strong Version of CAH that the previous proponents insisted on is not practical, but the weak version is more reasonable.

In sum, the behaviorist view of CAH proposed by Fries and Lado was particularly popular in the 1960s in SLA. Linguists who support behaviorist views regard language learning as the training of habits. Based on behaviorism, CAH is dedicated to detailed comparison of the similarities and differences between the native language of learners and the target language. It assumes that SLA is easy when the target language is similar to the native language, but difficult when the two are different. The similarities are thought to lead to positive transfer which facilitates SLA and different patterns which are predicted to lead to errors are known as negative transfer. CAH is expected to predict the errors second language learners with different language backgrounds make. However, CAH is refuted by many empirical findings. The research findings have shown that, many of the predicted errors due to the differences between the target language and native language had not occurred. Furthermore, many errors can not be explained by L1 transfer. It is clear that the learner's native language is not the only factor that influences SLA. Chomsky's argument (1959) of acquisition makes the habit-formation theories of language acquisition untenable, and as a result, the behaviorist perspective on language acquisition has been replaced by the mentalist perspective. The notion of transfer temporarily lost ground in the field of second language acquisition.

Contrastive Rhetoric (CR) is another hypothesis which emphasizes the negative transfer of native language. Initially introduced by the American applied linguist Robert Kaplan (1966), CR claims that the linguistic and rhetorical conventions of learners' native language will interfere with L2 writing. Connor defines CR as follows:

> Contrastive rhetoric is an area of research in second language acquisition that identifies problems in composition encountered by second language writers and, by referring to the rhetorical strategies of the first language, attempts to explain them.
>
> (Connor, 1996: 5)

CR maintains that writing is a cultural phenomenon and each language has rhetorical conventions unique to itself. CR emphasizes cultural difference in rhetorical patterns between different languages. It appeals to writing teachers and second language writing researchers and gained widespread popularity in 1970s. Many empirical studies were conducted (Kaplan, 1966, 1972, 1988, 1991; Kobayashi and Rinnert, 1996; Kobayashi and Rinnert, 2002, 2007) to investigate text organization patterns of students' writing or rhetorical differences and L1 to L2 rhetorical transfer.

At the same time, CR has received a great deal of criticism

for the following reasons: Firstly, CR takes cultural rhetoric as a static, exotic system instead of a fluid, dynamic historical process (Ostler, 2001; Kubota and Lehner, 2005). Secondly, CR overgeneralizes the L1 rhetoric from the investigation of students' L2 essays in college-level academic contexts (Hinds, 1983, 1987; Hirose, 2003). It neglects the fact that many other factors such as teaching methods and L2 proficiency may also impact on L2 textual features. Thirdly, CR fails to regard students as human individuals and their L1 is viewed as a deficiency (Kubota, 1992; Kubota and Lehner, 2004). It assumes that the students in their studies are homogeneous groups loyal to their cultural norms and transfer them to L2 writing. It also assumes that L1 rhetoric is problematic and will be negatively transferred to their L2 writing. This hypothesis overlooks the possibility of positive transfer, the fact that students' L1 language competence can facilitate their L2 learning.

2.1.1.2 Zero Transfer

The representative of non-transfer view is Creative Construction hypothesis (CC) which is based on cognitive science and mentalism. The proponents (Dulay and Burt, 1974a, 1974b; Corder, 1981; Bailey, Madden and Krashen, 1974) of CC argue that the acquisition of L2 is a process that is similar to the acquisition of the native language and it relies on the innate mental mechanism but not L1 transfer. Therefore L1 plays no role in SLA and language transfer does not exist. Corder (1981) claims that the starting point of SLA is the same as that of the native language, namely, the Universal Grammar. He asserts that language learners can construct an internal representation of language system with available language input and language acquisition device.

Dulay and Burt (1974a, 1974b) argue through experiments that L2 acquisition is a creative process which is similar to the acquisition of native language. They (1974a) conducted a study, including 55 Chinese and 60 Spanish students who studied English. It was found that the acquisition process of 11 morphemes was similar to that of the American students who studied English as their native language. Language learners made similar kinds of errors at the same learning stage despite their different native languages. They (1974b) classified and calculated the errors made by 179 Spanish English-learners and found that only 3 percent of the errors arose from the interference of their native language.

Minimalist position is another approach put forth by Dulay and Burt to play down the role of native language. The representatives are Dulay and Burt, Krashen and Klein. The proponents of minimalist position seek to emphasize the universal processes of language learning and deny language transfer. As noted above, Dulay and Burt (1974a, 1974b, 1975, 1977) made a series of empirical studies to test the effectiveness of CAH.

Krashen also minimizes the role of native language. He denies language transfer and takes language transfer from L1 to L2 as the ignorance of L2 knowledge. He asserts (1981: 67) that "the L1 may 'substitute' for the acquired L2 as an utterance initiator when the performer has to produce in the target language but has not acquired enough of the L2 to do this".

CC offers SLA research a cognitive perspective. According

to CC, SLA is a complicated process, and the cognition of the world and the inner cognitive device will affect the learning process. However, it lost the favor of linguists by completely denying the influence of native language and ignoring the factors of individual differences. The minimalist position neglects the role of L1 in L2 learning and emphasizes the importance of other factors. Gass (1988: 384) points out that it is "neither that everything is transferred nor that nothing is transferred". Therefore, the complete denial of language transfer has finally been proved to be untenable.

2.1.1.3 Positive Transfer

The third type is positive transfer that assumes that L2 learner's native language can facilitate SLA. Many studies (Cummins, 1982; Gass, 1979, 1983; Hyltenstam, 1984) have been conducted to prove how transfer has a facilitative effect. Three main hypotheses concerning positive transfer are introduced in the following part: Common Underlying Proficiency (CUP), The Full Access/Full Transfer Hypothesis (FA/FT) and Minimal Trees Hypothesis (MTH). These hypotheses are proposed on the basis of UG. According to UG, human beings contain an internalized set of rules for organizing language. In turn, it assumes that all languages have a common set of rules as the structural basis of all languages. The proponents of positive transfer attempt to seek out the common features between languages.

Cummins (2000: 38) theorizes CUP and defines it "the cognitive/academic proficiency that underlies academic performance in both languages". It means that language learners acquire the concepts when they are learning their first language, and those concepts are transferrable to the second language.

CUP claims that the cross-lingual proficiency depends on each other and enhances the cognitive and academic skills of both languages. It indicates the interdependence of concepts, skills and linguistic knowledge in a central processing system. Cummins (1982: 14) points out that "the fact that there is little relationship between amount of instructional time through the majority language and academic achievement in that language strongly suggests that L1 and L2 academic skills are interdependent". CUP is often symbolized visually by Dual Iceberg Representation (see Figure 2.1). It clearly shows that two icebergs represent the two languages that overlap and share, underneath the surface feature, a common underlying proficiency. In other words, languages are superficially distinct from each other but share some common concepts and knowledge under the water line.

Figure 2.1 Dual iceberg representation

The Full Access/Full Transfer Hypothesis (FA/FT) is proposed by Schwartz and Sprouse (1994, 1996) and by Dekydtspotter, Schwartz and Sprouse (2006). It is a model that seeks to answer the question of developmental stages of interlanguage. This model assumes that the initial state of SLA is constituted by the parameter settings of one's native language. FT indicates that the initial state of SLA is composed of the L1 grammar excluding specific lexical items. FA indicates that UG is fully accessed during L2 development when interlanguage is to be restructured, which makes it possible to reset parameters during the L2 acquisition.

The Minimal Trees Hypothesis (MTH) is proposed by Vainikka and Young-Scholten (1994, 1996a, 1996b). Similar to the FA/FT hypothesis, MTH holds that the initial state is the grammar based on the native language of the language learners. Different from the FA/FT hypothesis, MTH claims that only part of L1 grammars are used in the initial state. According to MTH, what L1 transfers into the L2 acquisition is merely confined to lexical projection, excluding functional categories which are available in the UG content. Functional categories will be acquired gradually while L2 input is exposed to the language learners. Therefore, the interlanguage development takes the form of a gradual development of functional structure.

The study of positive transfer goes largely unnoticed, and is less discussed in the study of SLA. There are several reasons for this. First, it is too difficult to summarize the highly abstract universal grammar which applies to all natural languages. Moreover, the researchers tend to study the errors made by language learners to investigate language transfer. They are prone to pay more attention to the differences between languages and negative transfer of native language.

2.1.2 Transfer of L1 and L2 in L3 Acquisition and Bi-directional Transfer

In recent years, researchers are interested not only in language transfer of native language in L2 acquisition but also in language transfer of L1 and L2 in L3 acquisition (Hammarberg, 2001; Cenoz, 2001; De Angelis and Selinker, 2001; Hüseyin, 2010) as well as the bi-directional transfer between the learner's native language and the target language (Ionin et al., 2013; Su, 2010, 2012).

Cenoz (2001) conducted a study to probe into the cross-linguistic influence of age and language typology on third language acquisition. The study was carried out in Basque Country where English, the third language, was taught. The participants were bilingual students of Spanish and Basque. By using a "Frog story", Cenoz explored how the L2 status and age affected the process of the third language acquisition. The experimental results showed that all the students presented a stronger influence from Spanish than from Basque. Both English and Spanish are Indo-European languages while Basque is a non-Indo-European language. Cenoz claims that linguistic distance plays a significant role in cross-linguistic transfer. Angelis and Selinker (2001) define the influence of a non-native language on another non-native language interlanguage transfer. They claim that language transfer is not comprehensive if it is based only on two languages.

Hüseyin (2010) also studied how to facilitate learning

German by making positive transfer from English among some Turkish students. A comparative study on articles between English and German was conducted and it was proved to be of greater use in teaching German to Turkish students whose native language had no articles. It was found that English, the first foreign language taught in Turkey, was apparently effective in serving as a language-bridge between German and Turkish. Hüseyin claims that English, taught as the second language, should also be taken into account while teaching German as a third language.

In addition to the investigation of L1 and L2 transfer to L3, the bi-directional transfer also arouses the interest of researchers. Tamar (2011) conducted an experiment to address the question whether L1 influence on L2 learners was similar to L2 influence on L1 of bilinguals. The performance of English-Spanish and Spanish-English bilinguals was compared to that of monolingual English controls. The experimental results showed that both bilingual groups processed bidirectional patterns of transfer.

Su (2010, 2012) also investigated the pragmatic transfer of Chinese EFL (English as a foreign language) learners in their apologizing behavior to address the issue of bi-directional language transfer in foreign language learning. The results of both studies showed that cross-linguistic influence occurred bi-directionally at the pragmatic level.

2.1.3 Summary of Language Transfer

The study of language transfer has long been an essential

and controversial topic in SLA and in applied linguistics. Under the influence of theoretical trends in different periods, language transfer has experienced several phases: its heyday in 1960s represented by the "stimulus-response" view and CAH; its decline in 1970s for the presence of early interlanguage studies and CC; and its regaining the attention of linguists under the impact of cognitive study of language transfer. The importance of language transfer in linguistic studies has been reassessed for several times. The study of language transfer tends to be more reasonable and objective. A consensus has been reached that native language does play an essential part in SLA but the question is when and how it affects the process. The aim of research on language transfer is not to explore whether native language is transferable any more, but rather to "seek to understand the constraints that govern which aspects of native language are transferred and the underlying principles which determine the transferability of native language information" (Gass, 1988: 384). Many researchers (Eckman, 1977; Zobl, 1983; Kellerman, 1977; Ellis, 1994, 1999) seek to identify the specific constraints that promote or inhibit language transfer. Ellis (1994) summarizes three constraints that affect language transfer: linguistic, psycholinguistic and sociolinguistic constraints. The three constraints are subdivided into six: language level, social factors, markedness, prototypicality, language distance and psychotypology and developmental factors respectively. "One of the strongest claims in recent research on transfer is that the transferability of different features depends on their degree of markedness." (Ellis, 1994: 319) This book attempts to investigate the transferability in article acquisition from the perspective of markedness. Therefore, the theoretical and experimental investigation of markedness will be introduced next.

2.2 Markedness

Markedness theory is an important theory of structural linguistics, initiated by the Prague School in the 1930s for the phonological study. The linguist Trubetzkoy (1931) first put forth the notion in his work *Phonologie et géographie linguistique* to distinguish the distinctive features. Greenburg (1966) establishes the concept of markedness as a language universal which is applicable to different linguistic aspects such as phonology, morphology and semantics. Later UG proposed by Chomsky (1981) offers the theoretical framework for further interpretation of markedness. He develops markedness in the field of generative linguistics and analyzes it under the framework of "principles and parameters". Jakobson (1984a, 1984b) applies markedness to morphosyntactic categories and semantics. The notion of markedness has since been extensively adopted by generative and typological approaches to linguistics. For the purpose of this study, a retrospective survey of the representative definitions of markedness will be carried out first.

2.2.1 Definition of Markedness

Before undertaking the more detailed analysis of

markedness, it needs to address a fundamental question of terminology. As mentioned above, the term "markedness" was initiated in the early 1930s by Trubetzkoy (1931) and has since then been developed by linguists in different aspects. Different scholars define markedness from different perspectives: formal definition, psychological definition and typological definition.

One of the most influential definitions of markedness derives from Chomsky's theory of UG. According to UG, language rules can be divided into the "core" and "periphery" part. As is shown in Figure 2. 2, the core rules refer to those more general, basic rules of language structure and the peripheral ones are not limited by universal rules and symbolize their special historical origins. The core rules are either unmarked or marked while the peripheral rules are all marked.

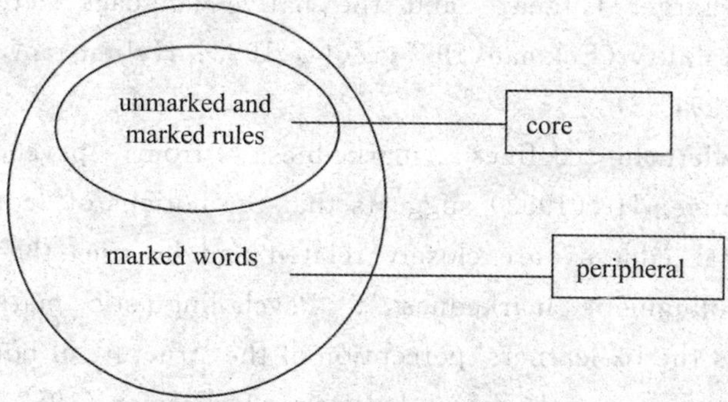

Figure 2. 2 Markedness in core and peripheral grammar

(cited in Ellis, 1999: 319)

The core rules reflect the common features of all languages, such as the word order, and the rules that are subject to the constraints of UG. The peripheral rules are unique to a particular language and free from the constraints of UG, reflecting the unique historical and cultural origins of the language. For example, the structure "the more... the more" is a peripheral rule that is unique to English. The markedness rank of the core rules depends on the parameters within the same category.

Ellis also defines markedness from linguistic point of view. He (1999: 319) stated that "some linguistic features are special in relation to others which are more 'basic'". Larsen-Freeman and Long (1991: 101) defines markedness "in terms of complexity, relatively infrequency of use and departure from something that is more basic, typical and canonical in a language". One of the important conclusions of the studies of language transfer is that the degree of markedness between forms of the target language and the native language determines transferability (Eckman, 1977; Zobl, 1983; Hyltenstam, 1984; Ellis, 1994).

Kellerman defines markedness from psychological perspective. He (1983) suggests that the notions of "coreness" and "markedness" are closely related and he uses the phrase "psycholinguistic markedness". Psycholinguistic markedness includes the L2 learners' perception of the structure of both their own language and the target language. Kellerman (1983) claims that adult native speakers have a sense of what is marked in their L1 that determines what is reliable to be transferred to L2. The learners will avoid transferring structures they perceive to be marked, which interact with their perception of the relatedness of languages. That is the reason why some L1 structures may transfer to some L2s but not to others.

Markedness is also a fundamental concept in typology. Croft (1990: 64) states in his book *Typology and Universal*: "markedness is an important tool for the topologist because it provides a means to directly link formal (structural) linguistic properties across languages". The typological concept of markedness lies in the asymmetrical and unequal grammatical properties of linguistic elements or conceptual structure.

Greenberg (1966) defines typological markedness as follows:

> A structure X is typologically marked relative to another structure, Y, (and Y is typologically unmarked relative to X) if every language that has X also has Y, but every language that has Y does not necessarily have X.
>
> (cited in Gundel et al., 1986: 108)

Eckman (1977) also puts forward a similar notion for typological markedness, proposing that the degree of difficulty in SLA corresponds to the notion of typological markedness.

> A phenomenon or structure X in some language is relatively more marked than some other phenomenon or structure Y if cross-linguistically the presence of X in a language implies the presence of Y, but the presence of Y does not imply the presence of X.
>
> (Eckman, 1977: 320)

Shen (1999) defines markedness as "a specific asymmetry phenomenon between elements of linguistic or conceptual structure" (Shen, 1999: 22). In these two contrastive linguistic elements, one is in the broader, dominant position known as the "unmarked" term and the other is the "marked" term. In other words, it is the characterization of a "normal" linguistic unit (i. e., the unmarked term) compared with a possible "irregular" unit (i. e., the marked term). An important task in typological study of markedness is to identify which properties are unmarked and which ones are marked.

According to the above definitions, typological markedness refers to an asymmetric and irreflexive relationship between linguistic structures across languages in the world. Under the view of typological markedness, the presence of a structure in one language implies the presence of its equivalent structure in another language, but not vice versa.

Ellis (1999: 417) also points out that "a typological approach to linguistic analysis involves a cross-linguistic comparison of specific features such as articles, word order or relative clause construction". Therefore, it provides a theoretical basis to identify which features are general ones and which ones are specific ones. It is generally accepted that the features that are more universal and appear in most languages are unmarked features, while those features that are specific in a particular language are marked ones.

Linguists define markedness from different perspectives and it is so controversial a definition that linguists hold different opinions on it. Many linguists have stated the vagueness of the concept. For instance, Ellis (1994: 323) admits it by saying that "one problem with work involving markedness is the vagueness of the concept". Eckman (1985: 306) acknowledges it by admitting that "one area in which more research is needed is in defining markedness relations". In spite of different views concerning the definition, there is no doubt that linguistic asymmetry phenomenon does exist no matter within a language or across languages. "Underlying all of the definitions is the notion that some linguistic features are 'special' in relation to others which are more 'basic'"(Ellis, 1999: 319).

From the above statement, we can see that there still lacks a consensus concerning the definition of markedness. In fact, it is not only the definition of markedness that has been a matter of debate, but the criteria for determining markedness as well.

2.2.2 The Criteria for Determining Markedness

Croft (1990: 71) states that "to say that one value in a grammatical category is marked and the other is unmarked subsumes a whole set of cross-linguistic patterns which should all behave in the same way, that is, every pattern should select the same value as the unmarked value. These patterns are the criteria for markedness". However, different scholars put forth different criteria for markedness from different aspects and determining what constitutes criteria for markedness relations remain a controversial area (Hume, 2011).

Greenberg (1966) applies markedness to typological linguistics and it is also a break from the tradition of Jakobson and Trubetzkoy. Greenberg takes frequency as the prominent factor of markedness in grammar suggesting that unmarked forms can be determined by the frequency of association of things in the real world. He also applies frequency to cross-linguistic comparison, suggesting that unmarked forms are those unmarked in a wide number of languages. Greenberg offers a most comprehensive statement of linguistic property for markedness. He (1966) summarizes the previous research, surveys markedness patterns of major grammatical items and integrates thirteen new criteria: five for phonological categories and eight for morphosyntactic categories.

Croft (1990) groups Greenberg's criteria into three: structural criterion, behavioral criterion, and frequency criterion, with behavioral criteria being divided into two types: inflectional behavior and distributional behavior:

> ⅰ. Structure criterion: the marked value of grammatical category will be expressed by at least as many morphemes as is the unmarked value of that category.
>
> ⅱ. Behavior (inflectional): if the marked value has a certain number of distinct forms in an inflectional paradigm, then the unmarked value will have at least as many distinct forms in the same paradigm.
>
> Behavior (distributional): if the marked value occurs in a certain number of distinct grammatical contexts (construction types), then the unmarked value will also occur in at least those contexts that the marked value occurs in.
>
> ⅲ. Frequency (textual): if a marked value occurs a certain number of times in frequency in a given text sample, then the unmarked value will occur at least as many times in a comparable text sample.
>
> (Croft, 1990: 187-188)

In addition to the intralinguistic evaluation, Croft expands the markedness patterns and defines cross-linguistic technique in behavioral criterion and frequency criterion:

> Behavior (cross-linguistic): if the marked value occurs in a certain

> number of distinct language types (represented by some orthogonal typology), then the unmarked value will occur in at least the language types that the marked value occurs in.
>
> Frequency (cross-linguistic): if a marked value occurs in a certain number of languages in a given text sample, then the unmarked value will occur at least as many languages in a comparable language sample.
>
> (Croft, 1990: 187-188)

Greenberg's criteria for markedness mainly focus on the evaluation of intralinguistic contrastive properties. It is impossible to explain the criteria of typological distribution by frequency. Croft mentions the cross-linguistic criteria for markedness patterns. Nevertheless, his criteria lack characteristics of cognition and communicative choices. Givon (1990) takes cognitive complexity into consideration. He (1995: 63) argues that "markedness is fundamentally an adaptive cognitive strategy for economy of processing. It tackles the potential random continuum of external reality with a strong innate bias, converting it into strongly asymmetrical cognitive dimensions". Therefore, he adds cognitive complexity into the criteria and puts forth three standards of markedness of discourse types:

> ⅰ. Structural complexity: the marked structure tends to be more complex or larger than the unmarked ones.
>
> ⅱ. Frequency distribution: the marked category (figure) tends to be less frequent, thus cognitively more salient, than the corresponding unmarked one (ground).
>
> ⅲ. Cognitive complexity: the marked categories tend to be cognitively more complex in terms of attention, mental effort or processing time than the unmarked one.
>
> (Givon, 1990: 947)

The study in this book takes Givon's criteria for markedness as the criteria for markedness degrees, since it includes both the structural and cognitive complexity which can explain the markedness relations more comprehensively.

2.2.3 Markedness in Language Transfer

It is widely acknowledged that markedness plays an important role in language transfer. Markedness is regarded as one of the significant factors which contribute to the transferability of the native language. The transferability depends on the corresponding degree of markedness between the native language and the target language. Studies on markedness and language transfer in SLA generally fall into the following two different categories: linguistic studies and psychological studies.

2.2.3.1 Linguistic Studies of Markedness and Language Transfer

Studies on markedness and language transfer at linguistic level in SLA mainly focus on the phonological, morphological and syntactic aspects. Only a few studies concern semantic features of markedness and language transfer. Representative studies of different aspects are discussed below.

Phonological linguists define markedness as distinctive features: the one with a certain feature is marked while the other one without is unmarked. Many phonological linguists (Major, 1996; Abrahamsson, 1999; Ashild, 2004; Yavaş, 2006; Yavaş and Barlow, 2006; Cardoso, 2007; Thomas, 2012; Hsu, 2013, etc.) are interested in markedness and language transfer at phonological level.

Major (1996) investigated language transfer and markedness by examining the acquisition of voicing contrasts among Korean learners of English. By examining the tokens of voiced and voiceless obstruent in initial, medial, and final position, Major found that Korean speakers correctly produced voiceless English obstruent in initial and final positions and experienced difficulty with voiced obstruent in final position. Major contributes the accuracy to the positive transfer and difficulty to the negative transfer of their native language. It was also found that the students' accuracy in initial position was higher than in medial position and the latter was higher than in final position. Major claims that the order of accuracy also supports the prediction of markedness before the experiment.

Cardoso (2007) investigated the effects of markedness and input frequency in the variable acquisition of /s/ plus consonant onset clusters in the speech of Brazilian Portuguese speakers learning English as a foreign language. Cardoso interviewed 10 Brazilian Portuguese speakers from two levels of English proficiency (i. e. , low intermediate and advanced). The results indicated that advanced learners tended to produce more target-like /s/ plus consonant sequences especially when the clusters were of the /sl/ or /sn/ type. By comparison, /st/ clusters had no significant effect on the production of /s/ plus consonant forms. It indicates that the sequence is only acquired at a later stage in the acquisition of /s/ plus consonant structure. Cardoso claims that markedness on sonority sequencing, not input frequency determines the order of acquisition of /s/ plus consonant clusters in second language speech.

Hsu (2013) made an experiment to investigate how the effect of language transfer and unmarkedness interact in Taiwanese EFL learners by using an Optimality Theoretic approach. His study focused on the nasals in syllable coda positions. The participants in his experiment included 29 Mandarin speakers and 33 Southern Min speakers. Each participant was required to read 51 test sentences with target coda nasals. Hsu summarized three findings: "(1) Southern Min speakers have less difficulty with English /m/ than Mandarin speakers do, suggesting a positive transfer of the first language (L1) phonemic system to the second language (L2); (2) there exists a strong tendency toward unmarked coronal /n/ in codas found in both Mandarin speakers and Southern Min speakers and there is no phonological rule of /m/ or /ŋ/ becoming /n/ in these learners' L1, revealing that an unmarkedness effect plays a significant role in shaping the production of interlanguage English with respect to coda nasals; and (3) the preceding two findings reveal that transfer and unmarkedness interact to influence the learning of English coda nasals and that unmarkedness overrides transfer in shaping Taiwanese EFL learners' interlanguage, leading to the strong preference for unmarked /n/ in phonetic representations" (Hsu, 2013: 64).

In morphology, linguists mainly focus on the complexity and simplicity of morphemes. Clahsen, Meisel and Pienemann (1983) examined the acquisition stages of German learners characterized by the absence or the emergence of five major word-order rules and argued that the order where the major rules emerged was invariable. Mazurkewich (1985) made a research to explore syntactic markedness in language acquisition. His study focused on the acquisition of dative structures and dative questions in a passive context in English. The participants in his research were French, Inuit (Eskimo) students as well as native English-speaking students. The data were interpreted within the framework of the theory of markedness and Case theory. The results showed that unmarked forms were acquired before marked ones, which were consistent with the predictions of the theory of markedness.

Hyltenstam (1978, 1984) studies the negative particles, the location of the verbs and the personal pronouns of attributive clause in sentences. He (1984) put forward a hypothesis: in the early stages of learners' interlanguage, the acquired form must be unmarked, regardless of the unmarkedness or markedness of the native and target language, because the unmarked forms are acquired earlier than the marked ones.

As is shown in Table 2.1, when the native language is marked, language transfer will not take place no matter whether the target language is marked or unmarked; when the native language is unmarked and target language is marked, language transfer will happen; when both the native language and the target language are unmarked, the interlanguage is also unmarked. Ellis (1999: 320) summaries two hypotheses concerning the influence of markedness on language transfer: (1) learners will transfer unmarked forms when the corresponding TL(target language) form is marked; and (2) learners will resist transferring marked forms, especially when the corresponding TL form is unmarked.

Table 2.1 Markedness and language transfer (Hyltenstam, 1984)

	Native language (L1)	*Target language* (L2)	*Early interlanguage* (IL)
1	unmarked	unmarked	unmarked
2	unmarked	marked	unmarked
3	marked	unmarked	unmarked
4	marked	marked	unmarked

However, White (1983, 1986, 1987b) conducted a series of experiments to investigate whether the marked forms can be transferred and had different findings. She reports that the French subjects in her experiment first acquired unmarked form, because French has the grammatical dative structure of pied-piping which is similar to that in English. She further indicates that the Inuit students took a different course in dative acquisition. They first acquired the marked form, because there was no special parameter in their native language that might interfere with the acquisition of the marked form. She states that the language form of the interlanguage in early stage depends not only on markedness, but also on the interaction of the learners' contact with the native language and target language. Sometimes learners may acquire the unmarked forms first, sometimes the marked forms first. It has been widely accepted that the unmarked forms in the native language will be transferred. As for whether the marked forms will be transferred, no consensus has been reached. It is one of the tasks in this book to investigate whether the marked forms in L1 will be transferred in the process of article acquisition.

Some researchers explore markedness and language transfer in semantic features. Liang (2011) studied markedness and language transfer in L2 acquisition of Mandarin classifiers by English and Japanese learners. Ionin et al. (2012) analyzed the intralinguistic markedness between the definite article *the* and demonstrative *that*. Alenizi (2013) investigated markedness and language transfer in the acquisition of the four non-generic uses of *the* by Arabic learners. The detail of these experimental results and findings will be further illustrated in the next chapter.

The investigation of markedness from various aspects of linguistic comparison between target language and native language offered experimental support for the markedness theory. Kellerman views the relationship between markedness and learning difficulty in a different way. Markedness for Kellerman has a psychological meaning.

2.2.3.2 Psychological Studies of Markedness and Language Transfer

As language learners will inevitably be influenced by their prior knowledge, the learning process definitely involves the psychological process in acquiring the target language. Therefore, mere studies of the linguistic markedness lack comprehensive understanding of language transfer. Kellerman puts forth psycholinguistic markedness and conducts a series of experiments to justify psycholinguistic markedness in transferability. According to Kellerman, language transfer is a complex decision-making process in which markedness plays the following roles:

> If the "markedness" level is too high, transfer will be blocked (characteristically language-specific items). If the "markedness" level is tolerable, it will be correlated with "language-distance". The interaction of the two factors will determine whether transfer goes ahead. The degree of markedness for any item is, of course, a constant since it is entirely NL-dependent.
>
> (Kellerman, 1979: 54)

Kellerman makes a series of empirical studies (1977, 1979, 1983, 1986, 1989) seeking to demonstrate that language learners can perceive the structures in their own language and judge that some structures are non-transferable and others transferable and this perception will affect what they really transfer. He (1979: 53) states that "there are three principal interacting factors which will control the use of transfer by a learner—his psychological structure of the NL (native language), his perception of NL-TL (target language) distance, and his actual knowledge of the TL".

The most famous of Kellerman's studies is his "breken" study in which he made a multidimensional scaling analysis to explore the dimensions and semantic space occupied by the verb "breken". The two dimensions are core/noncore and concrete/abstract. He chose native speakers but not L2 learners as his subjects. It was reported that the 17 sentences which contain "breken" were loosely related with the concrete/abstract rank order but closely with core/noncore. That indicates that native speakers' intuition can be used to predict the transferability. Kellerman suggests that learners' perceptions of what is transferable are independent of L2 proficiency. He contributes the native speakers' perceptions of the structure to the psycholinguistic markedness which he later defines as prototypicality. Ellis (1999: 326) summarizes Kellerman's experimental findings into three points: "The first is that it is possible to provide a clear operational definition of 'markedness' or 'prototypicality' by making use of native speakers' judgments of 'similarity'. The second is that learners have perceptions about what is transferable from their L1 and act in accordance with these perceptions. The third is that these perceptions reflect learners' ideas about what is prototypical or semantically transparent in their L1."

Another concept Kellerman (1977) uses to refer to learners' perceptions of markedness is psychotypology. It is regarded as another constraint to affect L1 transfer. Psychotypology refers to the learners' perceptions about language distance between the learner's native language and the target language. Kellerman claims that language learners all possess psychotypology, together with prototypicality, exert impacts and constraints on transferability. He holds that the learners' "prototypicality" determines what language learners are prepared to risk transferring and psychotypology determines what is actually transferred (cited in Ellis, 1999: 329). They interact with each other and influence language transfer together. What's more, they have no relationship with language learners' proficiency. It claims that the language learners have a sense of what is marked in their native language that tends to be transferred to the target language and they will avoid consciously or unconsciously transferring the structures that they perceive to be marked.

Their perception of the relatedness between the languages contributes to the fact that the structure of their native language may transfer to some target languages but not some others.

Rutherford (1982) has also applied the concept of markedness to language transfer. He summarizes linguistic and psycholinguistic constructs of markedness, points out the problem of markedness criteria and proposes to apply markedness theory to discourse. He suggests that the discourse features such as typological distance and presupposition can be further investigated and developed.

Givon (1990, 1995) applies markedness into cognitive linguistics. He (1995) argues that "markedness is fundamentally an adaptive cognitive strategy for economy of processing" (Givon, 1995: 63). He proposes the criterion of cognitive complexity and points out that the order of natural acquisition both in first language and second language reflects the order of cognitive complexity. The marked forms are considered cognitively more difficult to acquire than the unmarked forms. Givon (1995) puts forth three criteria: structural complexity, frequency complexity and cognitive complexity. He applies these criteria to the analyses of syntactic structure, such as clause types, nominal modalities, etc. Moreover, he also applies markedness to grammatical typology, analyzing the cognitive complexity cross-linguistically.

2.2.4 Markedness Differential Hypothesis (MDH)

The construct of markedness was initially studied in first language acquisition before being adopted by linguists in SLA.

Eckman (1977) proposed Markedness Differential Hypothesis (MDH) and introduced markedness into SLA. According to MDH, the degree of markedness is one of the constraints that affect transferability.

Similar to CAH, MDH also aims to find typological differences which constrain transferability. But different from CAH, MDH is based on the analysis of the markedness differences instead of language differences. CAH has provided helpful insights into the role of language transfer in SLA, but it cannot answer all questions. A brief comparison between MDH and CAH is introduced next to demonstrate how MDH can remedy problems of CAH and can account for language transfer more effectively.

The CAH under the guidance of behaviorism attributes all the learning difficulties in the interlanguage to the differences between the target language and the learners' native language, thus putting forward the hypothesis of "difference=difficulty". By comparing the language differences, CAH reckons to predict the interlanguage errors and the possible field of negative transfer. Empirical researches prove that the learning difficulties are caused by many different factors. In addition to language differences, they include the target language markedness, saliency of the target language, language learners' individual differences, language output and comprehension and so on.

In order to explain when markedness functions in the process of language transfer, Eckman (1977) revises CAH and proposes Markedness Differential Hypothesis (MDH), illustrating the markedness difference between the native language and the target language can predict the difficult areas of second language learners. He states that (1977: 61) "the areas of difficulty that a language learner will encounter can be predicted on the basis of a systematic comparison of the grammars of the native language, the target language and the markedness relations stated in Universal Grammar". The specific content of the hypothesis makes three predictions:

> i. Those areas of the target language which differ from the native language and are more marked than the native language will be difficult.
>
> ii. The relative degree of difficulty of the areas of the target language which are more marked than the native language will correspond to the relative degree of the markedness.
>
> iii. Those areas of the target language which are different from the native language, but are not more marked than the native language, will not be difficult.
>
> (Eckman, 1977: 321)

This proposal centers on the notions of typological markedness and implicational relations, therefore the notion of degree of difficulty corresponds to typological markedness. According to MDH, the interaction between markedness differences and language differences determines when language transfer happens: when the native language structure is unmarked, while the corresponding target language structure is marked, language transfer may happen; when the native language structure is marked, and the corresponding target language structure is not, language transfer is unlikely to happen. In other words, one of the conditions of language transfer is the different markedness of the second language rules.

The hypothesis can also be used to explain why SLA follows the general orders of language acquisition and why some language forms are acquired earlier than other forms. In general, learners acquire the unmarked forms first, and then the marked forms. As for why the marked ones are more difficult than the unmarked in the process of acquisition, Spolsky (1989) claims that markedness reflects the complexity of thinking, and Shen (1999) holds that the cognitive significance of the unmarked forms tend to attract our attention and they can be easily stored and retrieved and is closer to our expectations or anticipation. The significance of the markedness declines from the unmarked forms to the marked ones, thus increasing the difficulty of the acquisition gradually.

MDH attempts to specify markedness factors to reformulate CAH. Eckman (1985) points out that MDH varies from CAH in many different ways which can be concluded into three major aspects:

> The first major difference is that the MDH not only establishes the areas of difficulty between the NL and TL, but it also predicts the relative degree of difficulty between these areas.
> The second important difference between the MDH and the CAH is that the MDH allows for the possibility that certain differences between the NL and TL will not cause difficulty. Under the CAH, however, all differences are assumed to be a source of learning difficulty.
> This fact is related to the third important difference between the MDH and the CAH, namely, the predictions made by the MDH are in terms of relative degree of difficulty.
>
> (Eckman, 1985: 292)

Eckman believes that, different from CAH, MDH admits the necessity of the comparison between the native language and target language, but it is not powerful enough to predict the difficulties of learners. Therefore he introduces the notion of "relative degree of markedness" to predict learners' difficulties which must possess the common features, independent of any language.

Over the past three decades, a number of studies address the claims of MDH in SLA, especially in phonological study (Anderson, 1987; Carlisle, 1992; Zhu, 2004; Eckman, 2012). They mainly focus on the validity of markedness to explain the phonetic system in SLA. The experimental results show that typological markedness is a reliable factor to predicate the difficulties that L2 learners encounter.

Zhu (2004) examined the predictability of MDH by exploring American students' acquisition of Chinese initials. He proposes a hierarchy of difficulty for adult second language learners by applying markedness theory. He claims that the difficulty does not necessarily come from the differences between L1 and L2 proposed by CAH and the experimental results confirm the prediction of MDH.

Eckman (2012) summarizes the phonological studies in SLA and addresses several models and approaches to L2 phonology including MDH. He compares again the differences between MDH and CAH and lists representative studies (Anderson, 1987; Carlisle, 1992; De Jong et al., 2009) on phonology which address the claims of MDH.

As mentioned above, only a few studies concern the

semantic features of markedness and language transfer, and even fewer investigate the semantic features of articles from the perspective of markedness and language transfer. The study in this book attempts to explore when and how markedness constrains transferability.

2.2.5 Summary of Markedness Theory

The theory of markedness has been developed and improved since 1930s when the Prague School put forward the concept. The study of language transfer from the perspective of markedness breaks through the limitation of CAH and provides an opportunity to gain an insight into SLA in linguistic and cognitive respect. It can better explain and predict whether language transfer will happen and when it happens. It is beneficial to compare the differences between the native language and the target language and to predict possible difficult areas for language learners so as to reduce the learning difficulties in the process of SLA. The current study attempts to apply the theory of markedness and language transfer to the analysis of the English article system.

Markedness Theory has been widely applied to language transfer in SLA abroad, but few domestic studies have been conducted in experimental research. Moreover, the strongest explanatory power of markedness theory for language acquisition mainly lies in the levels of phonology, morphology and to some extent low-level of syntax. Only a few studies have been conducted to analyze the article acquisition. The previous studies on articles from perspective of language transfer and markedness will be introduced in Chapter 3. The present study attempts to investigate language transfer and markedness in the process of article acquisition at the semantic level. But before doing that, it is necessary to have a clear view of the studies of article acquisition.

Chapter 3 Studies on L2 Acquisition of English Articles

Lu and Fen (2001: 44) points out that "English articles are most commonly used words, but they are unstressed function words, hence perceptually non-salient and semantically light-weight". However, the use of articles in English is complex and context-specific and is by no means simple. The meanings of the same noun preceded by different articles can be different. Therefore, their importance in discourse and interactions and their complexity in the process of acquisition aroused much interest of many researchers. The article system has long been a hot topic among philosophers, linguists and psychologists. This chapter centers on the nominal domain of articles, linguistic and psychological studies on English articles at home and abroad, as well as the studies of language transfer and markedness in article acquisition. A comprehensive overview of previous studies related to English articles is given in order to shed light on subsequent research.

3.1 The Nominal Domain of Articles

Articles fall into the category of functional words that cannot be used independently. They can only be used in conjunction with nouns and form NPs to convey specific meanings. Therefore, it is necessary to look into some relevant referential properties of nouns to have a better understanding of article acquisition. Common nouns usually have two meanings: denotative meaning and referential meaning. The former is closely related with the conceptual connotation and the latter concerns the meaning that the speaker really wants to refer to. Of the two types of meanings, it is referential meaning of nouns that is closely related with the use of articles. Therefore, only the referential meaning of nouns is discussed here.

Stockwell et al. (1973) classifies NPs on the basis of definiteness and reference. They first grouped NPs into two types: definite and indefinite. Definite NPs refer to those both the speaker and the hearer know what the speaker is referring to. In English, the definite NPs are usually preceded by the definite article, demonstratives or possessives. Indefinite NPs includes specific and non-specific NPs preceded by an indefinite article or a zero article. Another approach that Stockwell et al. (1973) proposed to classify NPs is based on their reference. NPs can be either referential or non-referential. A referential NP, namely, a definite or a specific NP, has a particular referent. A non-referential NP, including indefinite and generic NPs, does not refer to any referent.

Tang (1988) further explores the relationship between NPs and their references in English. He suggests that English NPs can be divided into four types: (1) the proper noun, (2) the definite NP (the NP that is preceded by a definite article, a determiner, or the possessive NP), (3) the singular indefinite NP (a countable N preceded by an indefinite article *a*), and (4) the plural indefinite NP (a plural countable N preceded by ∅ or a singular uncountable N preceded by ∅) (cited in Hsin, 2002: 357). These four types of NPs in English represent five types of reference: definite reference, specific reference, generic reference, non-specific (or indefinite) reference, and non-referring reference. The first three types are definite references and the last two indefinite references.

As indicated above, the referential meanings of nouns can only be realized when they are used with articles, demonstratives, possessives and so on. To further investigate the referential meanings of nouns, Abney (1987) proposed Determiner Phrase Hypothesis (DP Hypothesis), an extended notion of NP.

3.1.1 DP Hypothesis

Chomsky (1986) proposes that function words should also project to the phrasal level like content words. Abney (1987) follows the line of Chomsky and advances the Determiner Phrase Hypothesis (DP Hypothesis). This hypothesis proposes that a phrase is headed by a determiner instead of a noun. DP is a syntactic category projected by the class of determiner elements.

According to DP Hypothesis, an NP belongs to a DP, and the noun is taken to be the complement of a determiner (Abney, 1987). Therefore, a DP is the functional superstructure of an NP and verb phrase. It is opposite to the traditional view that determiners belong to specifiers of NPs. The DP Hypothesis has gained ground in the field of linguistics and is now a dominant view in generative grammar. In the past two decades, the functional category of DP has aroused much interest in SLA (Abney, 1987; Hawkins et al., 2006; Robertson, 2000; Wakabayashi, 1997; White, 2003; Snape, 2007, etc.).

Following the proposal of Abney, Radford (1997) also claims that all the NPs are projections of a head determiner. He argues that DP is grammaticalization of the semantic feature of definiteness and bare nouns are DPs headed by a null determiner. Radford (2006) suggests that demonstratives can also function in DPs to refer to a definite referent in addition to the definite article *the*.

Wakabayashi (1997) made a comparative study of DPs between Japanese L2 learners whose native language has no article system and Spanish L2 learners whose native language has. He compared the two groups based on a grammaticality judgment task on the number feature of indefinite article *a/an* and plural bound morphemes. He reported that language transfer did not take place on Japanese learners. Wakabayashi explained that it was due to the lack of properties of the corresponding features of determiner and number in Japanese. He (1998) proposes Determiner Parameter which is either optional or obligatory. English and Spanish set the parameter of determiner and number in an obligatory way while Japanese learners optional. Therefore the Japanese learners acquire the specification of English determiners later than Spanish learners.

Snape (2007) investigated the typological differences of NPs and DPs between Spanish and Japanese. He took Nominal Mapping Parameter (NMP) and Article Choice Parameter (ACP) as the focus of his analysis and analyzed the licensing function of determiners and numbers in English and Spanish. It will be illustrated in detail in the part of the introduction to NMP. Ko et al. (2006, 2008) also explored universal semantic features of articles on the basis of DPs. They termed indefinite DPs in the set membership *partitivity* that will be introduced in semantic studies of articles in this chapter.

In this book, the comparison between L2 acquisition of English articles and other determiners will be investigated. Chinese lack articles, but there exist other determiner such as demonstratives like "zhege"(this), "nage" (that), "zhexie" (these), and "naxie"(those), possessives like "wode" (my), "nide" (your). These determiners can find their equivalents in English. A question arises: Is it more difficult for Chinese L2 English learners to acquire articles than to acquire other determiners? The answer to this question will be explored in Chapter 5.

3.1.2 The Nominal Mapping Parameter

As a parameterized property of UG, a model Nominal Mapping Parameter (NMP) was proposed by Chierchia (1998) as a means of distinguishing typological differences of nouns with regard to articles. In Chierchia' model, languages can be distinguished by two features: whether their NPs can function directly as arguments in syntactic expressions ([±argument] languages) and whether their NPs are predicates requiring a determiner to license them ([±predicate] languages). Therefore, the typological differences between languages can be captured through the use of binary features: [±argument] ([±arg]) and [±predicate] ([±pred]).

Some languages such as Chinese, Japanese and Thai lack article system, and there are no number marking on the nouns, therefore NPs in these languages can map onto arguments directly without the need for a determiner and be denoted as [+arg][−pred]. Some other languages such as Spanish, French, Italian and Greek have articles and the number marking on nouns is also necessary. The bare mass nouns, however, are not grammatically allowed in these languages. NPs in these languages need a determiner to turn them into arguments which can be denoted as [−arg][+pred]. English allows bare plurals and mass nouns to be arguments directly but countable singular nouns still need a determiner to turn them into argument to be grammatically correct. Therefore English is a language with the setting of [+arg][+pred].

Some researchers (Hawkins et al., 2006; Snape, 2007) test the setting and resetting of NMP through experimental and theoretical researches. Snape (2007) made a cross-linguistic analysis of NPs and DPs of Japanese and Spanish. It is a semantic and pragmatic comparison of determiner and number between Japanese and Spanish and the analysis of the usage of qualifiers and demonstratives. Based on the theoretical basis of UG and language transfer, Snape analyzed the licensing function of determiners and numbers in English and Spanish. Through a series of experiments, Snape discussed how NMP was related to the acquisition of NPs and DPs. The count-mass grammaticality judgment task showed that L1 Japanese learners and L1 Spanish learners both performed well and L1 Japanese learners wrongly rejected the grammatical mass context compared with L1 Spanish learners. Snape argued that it was due to different NMP settings and it suggested language transfer, "the Japanese learners overall performed well on the task as they were aware of the conceptual differences of what is countable versus what is uncountable in the L2"(Snape, 2007: 279). Snape attributed the findings to native language interference which could account for Japanese learners' failing to distinguish the count and mass nouns.

However, some other researchers question NMP and make experimental research to prove that the NMP can not be applied to many languages. For instance, Cheng and Sybesma (1999) and Sio (2006) argue that the NMP is not appropriate for the setting of Chinese and Tomioka (2003) and Muromatsu (2003) prove through experiments that the NMP is not available to Japanese etc. Through a contrastive study of plural-marking in Chinese, Korean and English, Lardiere (2009) also claims that the NMP is apparently of little use.

Despite controversy, NMP offers a way to make a cross-linguistic prediction for the acquisition of articles. The cross-linguistic distinction between languages that have articles and those that do not have is central to the nominal domain. In addition to the research concerning the nominal domain of articles, many theoretical and empirical studies of articles have been made from linguistic and psychological perspective.

3.2 Linguistic Studies of English Article Acquisition

A variety of approaches have been developed concerning different linguistic aspects of articles (Christopherson, 1939; Kramsky, 1972; Eckman, 1977; Hawkins, 1978; Huebner, 1983; Ionin et al., 2004, 2006, 2010, 2012; Trenkic, 2007, 2008; Yang and Ionin, 2008; Ionin, 2012) and linguists are mainly interested in forms and semantic features of articles. Studies on articles from linguistic perspective mainly center on the syntactic, semantic and pragmatic aspects of article acquisition.

3.2.1 Syntactic Aspect of Article Acquisition

Formal linguists mainly concern themselves with the presence or absence of syntactic features. Two representative hypotheses concerning syntactic features are introduced here: the Representational Deficit Hypothesis and the Missing Surface Inflection Hypothesis. Opinions of the two hypotheses differ as to whether UG is accessible (and, if so, to what extent) in SLA.

3.2.1.1 Representational Deficit Hypothesis

Some scholars argue for a basic difference between the

nature of L2 and L1, assuming the accessibility of UG in L1 acquisition but not in SLA. Others propose a less radical difference between the development of L1 and L2, namely, a partial UG access through L1. This proposal means that only the features instantiated in L1 are accessible to L2 learners. Syntactic features that are absent in L1 will not be accessible, and syntactic representations of L2 learners' interlanguage will never be target-like (Hawkins and Chan, 1997; Smith and Tsimpli, 1995; Franceschina, 2001; Hawkins, 2001, 2003). These positions are collectively known as the Representational Deficit Hypothesis (RDH) proposed by Hawkins (2003).

The RDH is first known as the Functional Features Hypothesis proposed by Hawkins and Chan (1997), motivated by a study made by Smith and Tsimpli (1995). It claims that if some properties of functional categories in UG parameter are not instantiated in the native language of learners, then some specific features will be defective or absent after critical period in SLA. RDH predicts that, in L2 acquisition of English articles, learners might be able to eventually set the Article Choice Parameter to the setting of definiteness but have difficulty persisting with resetting the Nominal Mapping Parameter. Proponents of RDH (Hawkins and Chan, 1997; Hawkins, 2000; Hawkins and Liszka, 2003) hold that L2 learners either have "partial access" to UG or fail to reset parameter settings and can not acquire some specific features of the second language owing to the deficit of some syntactic components.

RDH supports the idea that UG is inaccessible, and native language plays a vital role in the development of SLA. It is deemed to be impossible for L2 learners to acquire syntactic structures which do not exist in their native language. Therefore, for learners whose native language lacks article system, the syntactic features of interlanguage will never be target-like.

3.2.1.2 The Missing Surface Inflection Hypothesis

An opposite view argues against any syntactic deficit in L2 grammars, claiming full UG access in SLA which is not restricted by the learner's L1. It suggests that variability can be attributed to learners' learning difficulties in fully mapping specified abstract syntax to surface morphological forms (Haznedar and Schwartz, 1997; Prévost and White, 2000; White, 2003). That is the Missing Surface Inflection Hypothesis (MSIH) proposed by Prévost and White (2000).

MSIH was initially used to account for verb functional categories in SLA. It explores whether L2 learners made use of unconscious knowledge of the functional projections and features underlying tense and agreement. According to MSIH (Prevost and White, 2000), SLA presents a similar variability in tense and agreement morphologically to L1 acquisition. Within the framework of UG, the variability of inflectional morphology results from the difficulties of identifying the proper morphological surface form. MSIH argues that the inflection is absent at the surface morphological level rather than at the abstract syntactic level. It also holds that infinite forms are used to replace the finite ones and the default form of infinite verbs is the bare marker. When L2 learners have no idea of how to use verb forms, they will resort to a default form. White (2003) argues that MSIH is also applicable to account for the acquisition of functional categories. With respect to the L2 article acquisition, according to the MSIH, the functional categories should be present in SLA. If L2 learners can't acquire the target language, they tend to find a default form to complement it. For those language learners whose native language has no article system, such as Chinese, zero articles are the default form, and therefore they tend to exhibit more article omission.

Robertson (2000) studied the variability of the article system in Chinese learners of English. Research data were analyzed under the framework of UG, and it was concluded that the article variability was affected by three syntactic principles: determiner drop, information recoverability and lexical transfer. Therefore, he asserted that the article acquisition was accessible to the target language under the frame work of UG.

Trenkic (2007) addressed the causes of article variability in a different way and found different results. He compared thc article production between Serbian L2 English learners and a Turkish L2 English learner reported in Goad and White (2004). The comparison mainly focused on the learners' tendency to omit articles more in adjectivally pre-modified (Art + Adj + N) contexts than in non-modified contexts (Art + N). Trenkic reported the asymmetry both in learners' spoken and written production. He argued that the pattern of results was not consistent with models assuming target-like syntax. MSIH was found not to predict the surface inflections which might miss, and it only accounted for omissions if they happened to be found in learners' production. Trenkic suggested that variability was caused by processing limitations, and the production of misanalysed elements was not syntactically motivated but "pragmatically motivated by the perceived need to express the meaning they encode" (Trenkic, 2007: 321) and relied on general cognition.

According to MSIH, UG is accessible and it is not restricted by the native language of the learners. The variability of articles originates from the matching difficulties between syntactic features and morphological forms.

3.2.2 Semantic Aspect of Article Acquisition

Some researchers focus on the meaning and distribution of article system and study the semantic and discourse features of English articles. They claim that semantic and discourse features of NPs are main factors affecting the acquisition of English articles. Four theoretical studies concerning semantic features of English articles are introduced next. Biological Program Hypothesis and the Semantic Wheel Theory are based on the distinction of two binary discourse features of specific referent (SR) and hearer's knowledge (HK). The Fluctuation Hypothesis (FH) and the Article Choice Parameter (ACP) are based on the distinction of semantic features of definiteness, specificity and later partitivity.

3.2.2.1 Biological Program Hypothesis and the Semantic Wheel Theory

Bickerton (1981) proposes a most systematic analysis of English articles, Biological Program Hypothesis (BPH), which promotes the study of English articles in SLA. He notes that the uses of English articles are mainly constrained by the semantic features of NPs in discourse that possesses two binary discourse features: (1) whether the NP is a specific referent [±SR]; (2) whether the speaker assumes that the hearer has the knowledge to know the referent [±HK]. Therefore, Bickerton makes two distinctions. One is specific/non-specific distinction which concerns whether the noun phrase the speaker refers to is a specific one. The other is the distinction of presupposedness/non-presupposedness which identifies whether the references are assumed known by the hearer. Therefore the NPs can be classified into four classes: [+P+S], [−P+S], [+P−S], [−P−S] and the uses of the articles can be classified into these four classes. These two distinctions become two important parts in BPH, which offers a unique and systematic approach to the study of article system.

Huebner (1983) employs Bickerton's distinction of articles and proposes the Semantic Wheel based on the binary features: [±SR] and [±HK]. Huebner (1983, 1985) works out the Semantic Wheel in which NPs are divided into four basic semantic types (see Figure 3. 1). The first type is [−SR][+HK] (generics), in which the definite, indefinite and the zero article can be used; the second type is [+SR][+HK] (referential definites), in which the definite article is required; the third type [+SR][−HK] (referential indefinites) which includes indefinite articles and the zero article; and the fourth type is [−SR][−HK] (nonreferentials) in which indefinite articles or the zero article are called for.

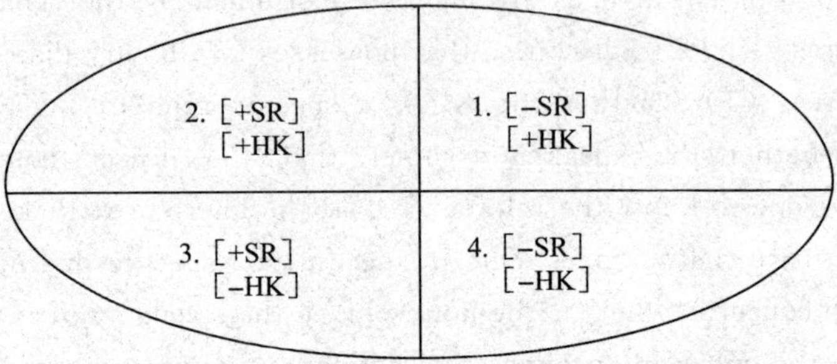

Figure 3.1 Bickerton's semantic wheel for noun phrase reference from Huebner (1983)

The above classification clearly pictures the semantic features of NPs in different discourses and referential constraints. With this classification, articles can be examined systematically and language learners' choice of different articles in different semantic contexts can be understood.

Parrish (1987) adopted Huebner's semantic wheel system and made a longitudinal study of a Japanese L2 learner's acquisition of article system whose language proficiency was at the "beginner level". He analyzed not only the article system, the use of *a/an*, *the* and ∅, but also the use of qualifiers and demonstratives for the reason that qualifiers and demonstratives can be used in the [+SR][−HK] and [−SR][−HK] contexts and demonstratives can be used in the [+SR][+HK] context. The study lasted for four months during which Parrish required the subject to tell stories about her own country and the US. The task was carried out every ten days and data were collected and classified according to the semantic features of [±SR] [±HK]. It was found that the subject's interlanguage of articles was not always target-like but to a great extent systematic and the systematicality was "found to be governed by the systematic functions of NPs, lexical categories and attempts to keep linguistically related forms consistent with one another" (Parrish, 1987: 381).

Tarone and Parrish (1988) again employed Huebner's distinction and discovered that different communicative functions that language played might cause variation in article usage. They investigated Japanese ESL (English as a second language) learners' acquisition of English articles to test whether the articles were acquired at the same time. 20 Japanese and 20 Arabic were randomly selected and were required to finish different tasks including a grammar test, an interview and a narrative task. The distribution of NPs and the accuracy of NPs with articles and pre-modifiers on the three tasks were collected and measured. It was found that the accuracy of the article system in the context of [+SR][−HK] was markedly lower than in [+SR][+HK] and [−SR][+HK] contexts and that the task-related variation in interlanguage was due to some complex factors. Tarone and Parrish concluded that three factors influenced the variation of the learners' interlanguage. They are "the communicative function of a feature, the linguistic environment of that feature and social/situational factors" (Tarone and Parrish, 1988: 37).

The Semantic Wheel became a theoretical basis for later study of the acquisition of English articles. Many other researchers (Master, 1987, 1988; Parrish, 1987; Tarone and Parrish, 1988; Thomas, 1989; Liu and Gleason, 2002) also studied the article acquisition in semantic respect, which contributes a lot to SLA study.

3.2.2.2 The Fluctuation Hypothesis and the Article Choice Parameter

In recent years, some researchers have replaced the classification scheme of [± SR][± HK] with [± definite] [±specific]. Ionin et al. (2004) defines definiteness and specificity. Definiteness means that "the speaker and the hearer presuppose the existence of a unique individual in the set denoted by the NP" and specificity means that "the speaker intends to refer to a unique individual in the set denoted by the NP and considers the individual to possess some noteworthy property" (Ionin et al., 2004: 5). They propose new theories on the article study: the Fluctuation Hypothesis and the Article Choice Parameter.

Following Fodor and Sag's (1982) proposal to set specificity as a semantic feature of articles and the contrastive studies of definiteness by Lyons (1999), Ionin et al. (2003, 2004) address the error patterns of L2 learners under the framework of UG and propose a semantic parameter, the Article Choice Parameter (ACP). Instead of the binary features of SR and HK proposed by the former researchers, ACP encodes two settings, the features of definiteness and specificity:

> The definiteness setting: articles are distinguished on the basis of definiteness.
>
> The specificity setting: articles are distinguished on the basis of specificity.
>
> (Ionin et al., 2004: 12)

The setting of definiteness reflects "the state of knowledge of both the speaker and the hearer", while the setting of specificity reflects "the state of knowledge of the speaker only" (Ionin et al., 2004: 5). It can be represented by Table 3.1.

Table 3.1 Cross-linguistic article setting: Two languages

Article system with definiteness setting

	+definite	–definite
+specific		
–specific		

Article system with specificity setting

	+definite	–definite
+specific		
–specific		

Ionin et al. (2004) argue that the choice of English articles is distinguished based on definiteness setting: *the* invariably denotes definiteness and *a/an* indefiniteness, regardless of specificity. Meanwhile, they hold that some other languages, such as Samoan, exemplify the specificity setting. The two articles in Samoan *le* and *se* are used in specific and non-specific contexts respectively, irrespective of definiteness.

According to the ACP, the parameter settings are available to L2 learners under the framework of UG. Ionin et al. (2004) suggest that L2 learners whose native language lacks articles may initially fluctuate between the two settings for the lack of sufficient input and the fluctuation may disappear with the L2 learners' increasing exposure to the target language. It is known as the Fluctuation Hypothesis (FH), and Ionin et al. summarize (2004) two features for this hypothesis:

a. L2 learners have full access to UG principles and parameter-settings.

b. L2 learners fluctuate between different parameter settings until the input leads them to set the parameter to the appropriate value.

(Ionin et al., 2004: 15)

FH assumes that the article choice will fluctuate between the two parameter-settings of ACP and the error patterns of L2 learners can be predicted. It predicts that L2 language learners can correctly use *the* in [+definite][+specific] context and *a* in [−definite][−specific] or [+specific][−definite] context. However, the specificity setting is also available in interlanguage for those whose native language has a specificity setting, so arises the overuse of *the* in [−definite][+specific] context and *a* in [+definite] [−specific] context. Table 3. 2 demonstrates the article choice in L2 English under FH.

Table 3. 2 Predictions for article choice in L2-English under FH

	[+definite] (Target: the)	[−definite] (Target: a)
[+specific]	correct use of *the*	<u>overuse of *the*</u>
[−specific]	<u>overuse of *a*</u>	overuse of *a*

(Ionin et al. , 2004)

ACP and FH have been widely used and heatedly debated since it was firstly proposed. Ting (2005) tested the FH with different participants, 8 Chinese and 5 Spanish speakers of English learners, to find whether the fluctuation occurred among the language learners whose native language has the article system. It was found that both the L1 Spanish speakers and L1 Chinese speakers performed in a similar way to the native speakers. In other words, both L1 Chinese speakers and L1 Spanish speakers did not fluctuate between definiteness and specificity in [− definite] [+ specific] and [+ definite] [−specific] contexts.

Hawkins et al. (2006) conducted a study and found that fluctuation between definiteness and specificity happened among intermediate Japanese L2 learners of English in [−definite] [+specific] singular and plural count noun contexts. Reid et al. (2006) also tested fluctuation in the use of *the* and *a* in both [−definite][+specific] and [+definite][−specific] singular count noun contexts among intermediate Japanese and Spanish L2 learners of English. It was found that the Japanese group fluctuated between definiteness and specificity in [−definite] [+specific] and [+definite] [−specific] contexts. The Spanish L2 learners performed as well as the native controls and performed as predicted no fluctuation.

Snape (2007) explained why L1 Chinese speakers outperformed L1 Japanese speakers in studies of both Hawkins et al. (2006) and Reid et al. (2006):

> "Although Mandarin Chinese has no syntactic head D (cf. Cheng and Sybesma, 1999), the universal cognitive/pragmatic categoıy of identifiability is in the process of being grammaticalized onto the lexical items which could be treated as equivalents of the definite and indefinite articles in English (i. e., *yi* 'one' = [− definite], *nei*① 'that' = [+definite]); definiteness as a grammatical category in terms of the binary morpho-syntactic feature [±definite] is in the process of being fully developed in the Mandarin Chinese language/lexicon (as opposed to the case of Japanese)."
>
> (Snape, 2007:138)

① *na* and *nei* are two polyphones which both function as demonstrative("that") in Chinese.

It was found in Snape's (2007) study that there existed fluctuation between definiteness and specificity in the process of acquisition among the Japanese groups, while the L1 Spanish learners did not fluctuate. Snape argued that Spanish, like English, was a language with articles marking definiteness but not specificity. Due to full transfer of their native language, the Spanish learners did not fluctuate as predicted. However, Japanese learners fluctuated between the two settings, and it was caused by the learners' wrong selection of English articles' features, rather than a failure to set a binary ACP.

Tryzna (2009) also examined ACP and tested the predictive power of FH. He carried out a field study of Samoan articles and found that the same specific article *le* could be used in three contexts: [+definite] [−specific], [+definite] [+specific] and [−definite] [+specific] and the non-specific article *se* was restricted to [+specific] [−definite] context. The experimental result is different from the claim of ACP that Samoan encodes specificity. Consequently, Tryzna (2009) claimed that ACP was not a parameter but a cross-linguistic generalization and suggested a reduced version of ACP. By examining the L2 English article by native speakers of Polish and Chinese, two articleless languages, Tryzna suggested that L2 English article use was better characterized by variability instead of fluctuation.

Dai and Wei (2008) conducted a study to explore semantic features of articles by Chinese L2 English learners. The study was conducted under framework of Ionin et al.'s (2004) ACP and FH. The test paper followed Snape's (2006) pattern. The results reported that the two groups did not show fluctuation between definiteness and specificity in using English articles. However, Ning (2009) made a similar study and obtained different results. Her study supported FH and it showed that the two groups fluctuated between definiteness and specificity.

It seems that the validity of ACP and FH is still a controversial issue. The classification of [±definite][±specific] and [±SR][±HK] both denote semantic features of articles. In addition to the similarities, the two approaches have some differences as well. The classification [±definite] [±specific] overlaps with the classification [±SR][±HK] in three aspects as is indicated in Table 3. 3.

Table 3. 3 The correspondence between [±definite][±specific] and [±SR][±HK]①

	[+definite]/[+HK]	[−definite]/[+HK]
[+specific]/[+SR]	the/the	a, an, ∅/a, an, ∅
[−specific]/[−SR]	the/the, a, an, ∅	a, an, ∅/a, an, ∅

As Table 3. 3 shows, the binary features of SR and HK correspond with the settings of definiteness and specificity in all three types (referential definites, referential indefinites, and nonreferentials) except the type of generics. In classification of [±SR][±HK], all the forms of articles can be used to refer to generics, while in [−specific] [+definite], only the definite article can be used. In other words, the classification scheme of [± definite][± specific] ignores the zero article in generics.

① Zhou (2007) also illustrated the correspondence between [± definite] [±specific] and [±SR][±HK] in his article to investigate overuse of the definite article in SLA.

Ionin et al. (2004) list some examples which belong to [−specific] [+definite]. However, some other researchers (Li and Thompson, 1981; Chen, 1987; Zhou, 2007) hold that these examples should be included into the type of [+ specific] [+definite]. This study makes no distinction between [±SR] [±HK] and [±definite][±specific], but in type of generics, [±SR][±HK] distinction is employed.

After making the distinction between two semantic parameters of definiteness and specificity, Ko et al. (2006) advance another notion, partitivity, to supplement the universal semantic features of articles. They test whether L2 learners can properly associate *the* with the presupposition of uniqueness and analyze the overuse of *the* among L1 and L2 learners. Ko et al. term indefinite DPs in the set membership *partitive*, and offer a definition as follows:

> If a DP is [+partitive], it denotes an individual that is a member of a set introduced by previous discourse (cf. Enç, 1991; Diesing, 1992).
>
> (Ko et al., 2006: 173)

They reach a conclusion that at least three independent semantic factors are influencing the article choice: definiteness, specificity, partitivity. These universal semantic features signify uniqueness of referent, speaker's intent to refer and set membership respectively. In other words, [±partitive] is also regarded as a semantic factor that affects the article choice besides [±definite][±specific].

Based on the study of Diesing in 1992, Ko et al. (2008) propose another concept, presuppositionality, "a semantic feature which makes reference to the presupposition of the speaker and the hearer concerning existence of a referent" (Ko et al., 2008: 121). They distinguish presuppositionality from definiteness with the former denoting "the presupposition of existence of a discourse referent" and the latter "the presupposition of existence of a unique referent" (Ko et al., 2008: 121).

> If DP of the form [D NP] is [+presuppositional], then the speaker assumes that the hearer shares the presupposition of the existence of a unique individual in the set denoted by NP.
>
> (Ko et al., 2008: 120)

Presuppositionality is similar to definiteness except the feature of uniqueness. Partitivity is classified as a sub-type of presuppositionality. Ko et al. (2010) investigated how the three factors of definiteness, specificity, and presuppositionality affected L2 English learners' article choice. Based on the experimental results, they argued that L2 English learners fluctuated in using the definite article to mark definiteness, specificity, and presuppositionality.

Yang and Ionin (2008) also investigated the semantic features of definiteness, specificity and partitivity. They explored not only semantic factors but also pragmatic factors contributing to the application of uniqueness in L2 English which will be explained in detail in pragmatic aspect of article acquisition.

3.2.3 Pragmatic Aspect of Article Acquisition

Leech (1981) holds that it is not enough to exclusively

explain the semantic aspect of articles, and pragmatic analyses need to be involved to have a comprehensive study of articles. Unlike semantics, which examines meaning that is conventional or "coded" in a given language, pragmatics studies how the transmission of meaning depends not only on structural and linguistic knowledge of the speaker and hearer, but also on the context of the utterance. The context includes any pre-existing knowledge about those involved, the inferred intent of the speaker, and other factors. Therefore, many researchers (Hawkins, 1978, 1991; Liu and Gleason, 2002; Trenkic, 2007, 2008; Žegarac, 2004) studied article acquisition from the perspective of pragmatics. They mainly focus on the pragmatic strategies and principles which affect the process of article acquisition.

Hawkins (1978, 1991) made thorough analyses of the meaning and use of English articles from pragmatic perspective. He emphasized the significance of existence and uniqueness of referents in determining definiteness. He applied contextually supplied pragmatic sets or P-sets and classified the nongeneric uses of the definite article into eight types: anaphoric use, visible situation use, immediate situation use, larger situation use relying on specific knowledge, larger situation use relying on general knowledge, associative anaphoric use, unfamiliar use in NPs with explanatory modifiers and unfamiliar use in NPs with unexplanatory modifiers. According to Hawkins, the definite article might be used on the basis of a discourse antecedent (anaphoric and associative anaphoric uses) and independent from the previous discourse (situational, unfamiliar with explanatory modifiers and unexplanatory modifier uses).

Hawkins's descriptive list of pragmatic uses of the definite article is rather complete. Liu and Gleason (2002) combined Hawkins's eight types and classified the uses of the definite article into four general types: cultural use, situation use, structural use and textual use. 128 students at several universities with 18 different native backgrounds participated in their study. The participants were classified into three groups according to their different language proficiency levels: low, immediate and advanced. The results showed that the four nongeneric uses posed different levels of difficulty on language learners and there existed significant differences between groups in omission of the definite article in cultural and situational uses. They reported the acquisition order of the four types of nongeneric uses of the definite article: situation use, structural use, textual use and then cultural use. They also suggested that the pedagogical instruction of the definite article should accordingly follow the natural order of acquisition.

Žegarac (2004) investigated the acquisition of the definite article under the framework of the relevance theory. He found that the acquisition of articles was influenced not only by the pragmatic rules of the native languages of the learners but also by the specific hypotheses and strategies of individual learners. For instance, the zero-article-as-default strategy affected the individual variation in use of articles between different learners.

Trenkic (2007, 2008) analyzed the article omission and substitution in second language production from pragmatic perspective, "analyzing articles as nominal modifiers rather than as grammatical elements whose *raison d'etre* is structural" (Trenkic, 2008: 1). She introduced a new variable of context, Explicitly Stated Knowledge (ESK). According to ESK, it is the analyses and the judgment of the context of NPs that affect language learners' selection of articles rather than the semantic features of definiteness. Therefore the substitution errors made by language learners are caused by ESK.

Yang and Ionin (2008) explored L2-English learners' different ways of establishing uniqueness in discourse. 65 Chinese learners of English and 27 adult native controls participated in it. Through an Acceptability Judgment Task, the participants were required to identify whether the test sentences were acceptable. It was found that Chinese learners whose native language lacked articles tended to overaccept *the* in previously mentioned context or association even when uniqueness was not established. Therefore Yang and Ionin claimed that the Chinese learners' sensitivity to the semantic definiteness is closely tied to the pragmatic context.

3.3 Cognitive Studies of English Article Acquisition

In addition to linguistic studies mentioned above, some researchers (Bresson, 1974; Brown, 1973; Warden, 1976; Garton, 1983; Mizuno, 1985, 1999; Butler, 2002; Lee, 2013) studied the article system from cognitive perspective, focusing on psycholinguistic and metalinguistic approaches to article system and claimed that cognitive constraints were main factors contributing to the errors made by L2 learners in the acquisition of English articles.

Mizuno (1985) examined the process of interlanguage development in Japanese learners of English. 353 subjects were divided into 9 groups according to their English proficiency. He analyzed the reasons for them to make errors in article uses and classified the errors into five types: co-occurrence errors, word-order errors, overextension errors, underextension errors and substitution errors. It was found that the number of co-occurrence and word-order errors declined dramatically when the proficiency of the learners reached Level Three. The underextension and substitution errors apparently dropped from level one to four, but persisted in interlanguage till Level Nine. The overextension errors were main errors above Level Four and persisted in the interlanguage until Level Nine. Mizuno claimed that Japanese learners demonstrated the following five constraints in cognitive aspect:

> ⅰ. confusion between the concept of zero and nil.
>
> ⅱ. ignorance of the concept of the zero article in English.
>
> ⅲ. a lack of awareness of the boundary between the discrete and continuous attributes of nouns.
>
> ⅳ. limited opportunity for practice and exposure to meaningful expressions in English and the authentic rhythms of English in everyday life.
>
> ⅴ. a complete lack of awareness of deictic factors which constrain the article used.
>
> (cited in Mizuno, 1999: 127)

Mizuno (1999) also conducted a study and analyzed the interlanguage of the English article system from cognitive perspective. Nearly 2,000 Japanese EFL students from seven universities were chosen as the subjects of the study. This study summarized the findings of Mizuno (1985) with respect to errors in the English article system among Japanese learners, made use of the five types of errors claimed by Mizuno and examined from the same perspective with new data, expecting the subjects to demonstrate the constraints claimed by Mizuno. The data of five experiments supported the claims of Mizuno (1985) in terms of the use of articles: "cooccurrence and word-order errors sharply decreased at the early intermediate level; underextension errors were predominant even at the intermediate and the advanced levels; overextension errors were predominant even at the early intermediate level and the substitution errors began to decrease at the early intermediate level" (Mizuno, 1999: 134). The results supported the claims of the five constraints made by Mizuno (1985). At the same time, he offered the reasons why the native speakers could acquire articles easily and smoothly while Japanese adult learners could not. "The reason is that the articles are not merely elements which follow mechanical linguistic rules, but are deeply involved in psychological process of native speakers of English." (Mizuno, 1999:134)

Butler (2002) investigated the metalinguistic knowledge of the English article system that learners employed when they selected articles to "better understand the process of 'making sense' of the article system by learners who are at different stages in their interlanguage development" (Butler, 2002: 451). He selected 80 Japanese college students with different English proficiency as the subjects in his study. With a fill-in-the-article test and a structured interview, he investigated the reasons for the students to make article choices. Through a series of quantitative and qualitative analyses, he revealed conceptual differences with respect to the participants' inner perception of the factors of SR and HK together with their knowledge of countability. He concluded that there existed a clear difference in metalinguistic knowledge of the English article system by language learners with different language proficiency to detect SR and HK in dynamic contexts. Furthermore, even the higher proficiency learners had difficulty to properly detect HK and noun countability.

Lee (2013) also probed into metalinguistic awareness of Korean learners in article acquisition. 30 Korean and 5 native English speakers needed to finish a blank-filling task with English articles. The participants were divided into three groups according to their different proficiency: beginners, intermediate and advanced groups. As they were filling the blanks, they were required to verbalize reasons for them to make the choices in a think-aloud protocol. It was reported that the beginners tended to depend more on explicit knowledge and seemed to apply article rules that they could find in English grammar books. The advanced participants utilized more frequently implicit knowledge and made choices based on intuitive judgments. Lee claimed that concept with respect to article uses changed along with the increasing exposure to the target language and the overall language proficiency.

The above review of linguistic and cognitive studies on article acquisition shows that research in this field is active.

Some are interested in the referential meaning of NPs based on semantic features; some are intrigued by the development of articles and carried out longitudinal studies to examine the acquisition order of articles. Some others concern themselves with cross-linguistic studies of article acquisition and pay more attention to language transfer and markedness in article acquisition.

3.4 The Study of Language Transfer and Markedness in Article Acquisition

The theory of UG claims that the process of children's language acquisition is determined by a biologically endowed inborn faculty of language in children's brain. It suggests that linguistic ability manifests itself without being taught, which provides children with a genetic ability to acquire language without difficulty. Chomsky's UG aroused researchers' interest in language transfer and diverse standpoints have emerged ranging from full transfer (Schwartz and Sprouse, 1994, 1996) to no L1 transfer (Flynn, 1987; Epstein, Flynn and Martohardjono, 1996). White (2000) summarizes five approaches to language transfer. The five approaches are: (1) full transfer/partial access; (2) no transfer/partial access; (3) full transfer/full access; (4) partial transfer/full access; and (5) partial transfer/partial access.

Different theoretical standpoints determine different research methods as well as different results. In general, the experimental results have shown that subjects without articles in their native languages, such as Japanese and Chinese spend longer time to acquire the article system than those with articles in their L1s (Master, 1987, 1988, 1997; Gilbert, 1983; Thomas, 1989; Liu and Gleason, 2002; Snape, 2007; Crompton, 2011, etc.).

Gilbert (1983) investigated the acquisition of German definite articles by some foreign workers with different language backgrounds. Gilbert predicted according to transfer theory that those workers whose native language have the corresponding form of definite article (i. e., Spanish, Italian, Greek and Portuguese) would have a better performance than those not (i. e., Turks and Yugoslavs). It was found that the workers with native languages having definite articles used more definite articles as predicted. Moreover, they were found to learn an item more easily in L2 that is equivalent to one existing in their own native language. Zobl (1982) examined the differences in developmental routes of the definite article between Spanish and Italian learners with their native languages having definite articles and Chinese learners whose native language does not. It showed that the learners exhibited better control of L2 structures when their L1 possessed a similar structure and acquired them more rapidly. Furthermore, Spanish and Italian learners were found to move directly from the zero representation to the target form, while Chinese learners followed a different developing route: a demonstrative pronoun was employed first to mark the definiteness in the target language.

Crompton (2011) explored language transfer in article acquisition by tertiary-level L1 Arabic speakers in a corpus of

English writing. Frequencies of errors with articles were compared with those in native English and non-native English speaker corpora. It was found that overuse of the definite article for generic reference was among the commonest errors and Crompton argues that the strong likelihood is that these errors are caused by L1 transfer instead of the interlanguage developmental order.

Isabelli-García and Slough (2012) conducted a study to explore the acquisition of the non-generic uses of the English definite article by some Chilean L2 learners. The participants were required to complete a questionnaire containing deleted obligatory uses of *the*. They demonstrated different accuracy rates in the use of the definite article that were classified into four different types. Of the four types, the one the most similar to the learners' native language was the least difficult to acquire and the most different from the learners' native language turned out to be the most difficult. Isabelli-García and Slough explained that L1 rules were transferred to the L2 in the process of acquiring the definite article.

However, not all the researchers reported supportive results. Wakabayashi (1997) conducted a comparative study between Japanese and Spanish learners of English on the article acquisition in order to investigate whether Japanese learners of English would transfer optional setting to their interlanguage. He reported that language transfer did not happen among Japanese learners whose native language had no properties of the corresponding features of determiner and number. And the same result was also found in his study in 1998. Wakabayashi (1998) asked 55 Japanese learners to finish a gap-filling task with definite article or indefinite article. He hypothesized that Japanese learners would transfer the demonstrative *sono* (that) in Japanese to their interlanguage while acquiring the definite article *the* in the early stage of acquisition. The result of the experiment showed that the Japanese L2 learners acquired more successfully the definite article before singular NPs than the uncountable NPs. It was also found that the Japanese L2 learners did not transfer the demonstrative *sono* in their native language into their interlanguage. Wakabayashi explained that "the definite article is not only associated with the [+ definite] but also with the number feature of the noun phrase" (1998: 103). He drew the conclusion that Japanese learners had difficulty in acquiring certain pragmatic usage of definite article in some given contexts.

Many a research has been made to examine language transfer in article acquisition, but studies on article acquisition from the perspective of markedness are few in quantity, which is why this book finds it necessary to pay more attention to this topic. As one of the important approaches affecting the transferability of L1, the role of markedness in the process of acquisition should naturally be taken into account. Different from CAH, which simply hypothesizes "difference = difficulty", markedness theory claims that the interaction between markedness differences and language differences jointly determine when language transfer happens. The transferability depends on the corresponding degree of markedness between the native language and the target language. The unresolved issue of language transfer is also approached in light of markedness. In general, it is accepted that unmarked forms are transferrable, but whether marked forms are subject to transfer is still a controversial issue. The influence of language transfer and markedness in article system acquisition is supported or questioned by some researchers through different experimental results. However, studies on language transfer and markedness in article acquisition are few. The limited number of studies mainly focuses on intralinguistic markedness and language transfer.

Liang (2011) investigated markedness and language transfer in L2 acquisition of Mandarin classifiers by English and Japanese learners. English is a non-classifier language and Japanese a classifier language. Both Mandarin and Japanese have classifier system to demonstrate the mass/count distinction and nouns are classified based on semantic features. Liang made a distinction between classifiers and measure words, stating that classifiers were marked and measure words unmarked in that the former were considered less frequent cross-linguistically and more complex syntactically. Through an acceptability judgment test, it was found that unmarked forms were subject to L1 transfer in early L2 acquisition of Mandarin classifiers, while the marked forms were not. In other words, marked forms were found less transferable than unmarked forms in L2 grammar.

Ionin et al. (2012) tested how L2 Korean learners of English distinguished between English definite descriptions and demonstrative descriptions. Korean lacks articles, but it possesses demonstratives. It was hypothesized that transfer would lead the participants to equate definite article with demonstratives. Ionin et al. announced the necessity for the learners to know markedness between *the* and *that*. Ionin et al. (2012: 77) mentioned that "in order to differentiate between *the* and *that*, learners need: to learn that *the* is the unmarked, default option for indicating uniqueness and *that* is the marked, non-default option; and to make use of the markedness relationship between *the* and *that*..." The results showed that Korean learners' interpretation for definite descriptions was influenced by the semantic features of demonstrative descriptions in their L1. Ionin et al. suggested that L2 learners' acquisition of articles could be influenced by transfer from a closely related category.

Alenizi (2013) investigated the acquisition of the English definite article *the* by Arabic learners of English. The study mainly focused on four non-generic uses of *the* including textual use, situational use, cultural use and structural use. The aim of the study was to find evidence to support CAH, language transfer and MDH. It was found that the situational use of the definite article yielded the highest accuracy among the four types. This finding supported the prediction of CAH which claimed that the linguistic features that were similar between L1 and L2 would be easier to acquire than those that were different. Furthermore, the situational use of *the* also presented a positive transfer in that the participants transferred their L1 use and thus achieved higher level of accuracy. MDH also found support in this study. MDH is considered to be complementary to CAH. According to MDH, the degree of difficulty in the acquisition depends on the comparative markedness of a certain linguistic feature. Alenizi analyzed the intralinguitsic markedness between the anaphoric and the associative anaphoric functions of *the* within the textual use. Based on the frequency of occurrence, he claimed that both of the two functions seemed to be unmarked in English. However, the associative anaphoric function seemed to be more marked than the anaphoric one in Arabic. The experimental results showed that the errors in the more marked associative use greatly outnumbered the errors in less marked anaphoric use.

The above review shows extensive research on English articles at home and abroad. However, the investigation of article acquisition under the framework of markedness and language transfer is a very under-researched area in SLA. Only a relatively few studies focus on intralinguistic markedness of articles. Virtually no attention has been paid to interlinguistic markedness and language transfer in article acquisition. Findings of previous studies offer some insight into different aspects of the present study to explore the semantic features of NPs and typological differences in markedness and to investigate when and how language transfer takes place to affect the article acquisition.

Based on the previous studies mentioned above, this book attempts to explore the article acquisition under the framework of markedness and language transfer. The subsequent experiments in this book are reported and discussed in the next two chapters. The typological and semantic differences between Spanish, French, languages with an article system and Chinese, a language without article system are analyzed in Chapter 4. The overuse/underuse of articles will be dealt with in Chapter 5. In addition to the experiments, the cognitive process and metalinguistic knowledge of article acquisition will also be reported in Chapter 6. All the experiments aim to investigate when and how markedness and language transfer function in article acquisition in the hope that the researcher may uncover the reasons which hinder Chinese learners' acquisition of articles and may develop some effective methods to assist them in acquiring the English article system successfully.

Chapter 4　Experiment 1: The Multiple-choice Task

The literature review introduced the theoretical and empirical studies on language transfer, markedness and article acquisition in SLA, which paved the way for the study in this chapter. The aim of this chapter is to investigate the differences between language learners whose native language has an article system and Chinese L2 learners whose native language has no article system. Three research questions are addressed in this experiment. A detailed description of the methodology is given. It includes such aspects as the subjects, analytical methods, semantic types of articles, and the procedure of the experiment. The experimental results are presented and analyzed from the perspective of markedness and language transfer.

4.1　Research Questions

As reviewed in Chapter 3, previous empirical studies investigated the role of language transfer in L2 article acquisition through analyzing the semantic and syntactic features of articles. This experiment aims to find when language transfer happens and to explore the relationship between markedness and language transfer in the process of article acquisition. The following research questions are to be addressed:

(1) Will language learners' native language affect their performance?

(2) Are there significant differences between language learners in terms of different semantic article types?

(3) When does language transfer happen due to markedness in article acquisition?

In order to explore the answers to the above questions, the author selected French and Spanish English learners whose native languages have an article system, Chinese English learners whose native languages have no article system as well as native English speakers as the subjects of the experiment. It aims to explore whether the language learners' native language will affect their performance in different semantic types of article acquisition and whether language transfer will occur based on different degrees of markedness.

4.2 Research Method

4.2.1 Participants

The participants were 43 students majoring in Finance in University of Central Lancashire (UCLan) in the UK, including 6 French, 6 Spanish, 19 Chinese English learners and 12 native English speakers. The non-native speakers had studied in UCLan for less than a year when the experiment was conducted. They had studied English in their home country for 8-10 years. The participants were divided into 4 groups according to their different native languages. The basic information of the participants is listed in Table 4. 1.

Table 4. 1 Participants in the experiment

Group	L1	Age	Number	Exposure to English study
Group 1	English	19—21	12	19—21 years
Group 2	French	20—22	6	11—12 years
Group 3	Spanish	19—25	6	8—12 years
Group 4	Chinese	18—21	19	10—13 years

4. 2. 2 Semantic Types of Articles

The articles in this experiment were classified into four semantic types: generics ([−SR][+HK]), referential definites ([+SR][+HK]), referential indefinites ([+SR][−HK]) and nonreferentials ([−SR][−HK]). The classification borrowed Huebner's (1983, 1985) Semantic Wheel for NPs reference.

Huebner's semantic wheel itself was based on Bickerton's (1981) Semantic Wheel Model. He classifies articles on the basis of the binary features of specific reference ([±SR]) and hearer's knowledge ([±HK]). Huebner further specified the subtypes of the reference according to the detailed semantic context of the NPs. Huebner's classification of articles captured the main relationships between the references and the noun phrases and has been widely adopted in studies of article acquisition for classifying NPs.

However, Huebner's classification of NPs is defective. For instance, Huebner holds that only the definite article *the* has the semantic function of referential definites, but the author finds that the zero article can also exert the same function in the context of [+SR][+HK]. For example, in the following sentence, "________ *Boxing Day, when Christmas boxes used to be given to servants, is the day following* ________ *Christmas Day.*", the proper NPs *Boxing Day* and *Christmas Day* are referential definites but are expressed with zero article. Therefore, the author adds some subtypes according to the article forms and their referential meanings such as the following:

T1. The referential definite [+SR][+HK]

T1S1. Specific referents assumed known to the hearer

T1S2. Referent previously mentioned in the discourse

T1S3. Unique referent or conventionally assumed unique referent

a) Definite article "the" to refer to the unique referent

b) Zero article to refer to the unique referent

c) "the" before the ordinal number and superlative degree of adjectives

T1S4. Referent physically present

T2. The generics [−SR][+HK]

T2S1. a) Definite article

b) Indefinite articles

c) Zero article

T2S2. the+*adj*.

T3. The referential indefinites [+SR][−HK]

T3S1. The weak version of "one"

T3S2. First mention of the [+SR] NP which is assumed not known to the hearer

T3S3. First mention of [+SR] NP following existential *have* and assumed not known to the hearer

T4. The nonreferentials [−SR][−HK]

T4S1. Equative noun phrases

T4S2. Conventional use

T4S3. Indefinite article to refer to price, speed, ratio, etc., meaning "every", "per"

4.2.3 Analytical Methods

The scores are analyzed with Analysis of Variance (ANOVA) to determine whether there exist significant differences between the mean scores of the four groups with different native languages and between the mean scores of different semantic types. All the statistics are analyzed by using the statistic software Statistical Package for the Social Sciences (SPSS 17.0). P values of 0.5 or lower are considered to be statistically significant.

4.2.4 Procedure

The experiment was conducted in October, 2011 in UCLan. The participants were asked to finish a multiple-choice task (see Appendix A). There are 45 items in this experiment. Each item is a multiple-choice question with four options of *a*, *an*, *the*, and

∅, and each correct choice generates one score. The participants were asked to choose the most appropriate one to each item. According to the classification of semantic types in the above section, each subtype consists of three items and all the items were selected from the National College Entrance Examination (NCEE) or mock exams of the NCEE.

The experiment was administered by the author and a professor in UCLan and it lasted for two class hours, 45 minutes each. The data were collected and statistical analyses were made by the author to explore the difference between groups.

4.3 Results

4.3.1 Comparison of Mean Scores between Different Groups

The accuracy of different groups is shown in Table 4.2. It shows that native English speakers scored higher than the other groups. With the total score of 45, the mean score of native English speakers was 41.5, 27.37% above the population mean. Mean scores of French and Spanish L2 learners were 34.17 and 33.17 respectively, 4.87% and 1.8% higher than the population mean. The mean score of Chinese English learners was 26.26, 19.39% lower than the population mean. The above descriptive statistics of mean scores indicate that there was discrimination validity between the language learners with different native languages.

Table 4.2　　　Accuracy of each group

Groups	Types	T1	T2	T3	T4	Total	Above the average
Group 1 (British)	[+ART]	19.58	5.33	8.25	8.33	41.50	27.37%
Group 2 (French)	[+ART]	15.83	4.50	6.67	7.17	34.17	4.87%
Group 3 (Spanish)	[+ART]	14.83	3.67	7.33	7.33	33.17	1.80%
Group 4 (Chinese)	[−ART]	12.00	3.21	4.21	6.84	26.26	−19.39%
Average Score		15.05	4.05	6.12	7.37	32.58	

Table 4.2 shows that the [+ART] group outperformed the [−ART] group, but a one-way variance analysis (ANOVA) was needed to see whether the four groups of participants' performance were statistically different. Before ANOVA, the test for homogeneity of variance for the above descriptive statistics was first carried out to test whether the population variances were equal.

Table 4.3　　　Test for homogeneity of variances

Total

Levene Statistic	df1	df2	Sig.
2.517	3	39	0.072

Table 4.3 shows that the testing P-value of Levene's test was 0.072, higher than the critical value (0.05). Therefore, the

obtained differences in sample variances were likely to have occurred based on random sampling from a population with equal variances. It indicates the availability to make the statistical data variance analysis.

Table 4.4 ANOVA between the four groups

	Sum of Squares	df	Mean Square	F	Sig.
Between Groups	1730.114	3	576.705	24.385	0.000
Within Group	922.351	39	23.650		
Total	2652.465	42			

Results of the one-way ANOVA show that there was significant difference ($F=24.385$, $p=0.000$) between the four groups' mean scores. In other words, there existed significant difference between at least two of the groups. As for between which two groups the significant difference existed, further analysis of the data was needed. Therefore, post hoc test of variance between groups with different native language backgrounds was carried out. Different letters were employed for the abbreviation of the participants' native languages (N stands for native English speakers, F for French, S for Spanish and C for Chinese). Table 4.4 presents Tukey HSD multiple comparisons between different groups.

Table 4.5 Post hoc test of the accuracy of four groups

(I) no	(J) no	Mean Difference (I-J)	Std. Error	Sig.	95% Confidence Interval	
					Lower Bound	Upper Bound
N	F	7.333*	2.432	0.022	0.81	13.86
	S	8.333*	2.432	0.008	1.81	14.86
	C	15.237*	1.793	0.000	10.43	20.05
F	N	−7.333*	2.432	0.022	−13.86	−0.81
	S	1.000	2.808	0.984	−6.53	8.53
	C	7.904*	2.277	0.007	1.79	14.01
S	N	−8.333*	2.432	0.008	−14.86	−1.81
	F	−1.000	2.808	0.984	−8.53	6.53
	C	6.904*	2.277	0.022	0.79	13.01
C	N	−15.237*	1.793	0.000	−20.05	−10.43
	F	−7.904*	2.277	0.007	−14.01	−1.79
	S	−6.904*	2.277	0.022	−13.01	−0.79

* The mean difference is significant at the 0.05 level.

Table 4.5 shows the accuracy of language learners with different native languages. At the significance level of 0.05, there existed significant difference (p = 0.000, 0.022, 0.008 respectively) between the native English speakers and the non-native speakers (Chinese, French and Spanish learners). The native English speakers significantly outperformed the non-native speakers no matter whether their native languages contain article system or not. The significant difference also existed between French and Spanish English learners whose native language has an article system and Chinese English learners whose native language has no article system (p=0.007, 0.022). As for the comparison between the mean scores of Spanish and French, no significant difference (p=0.984) was found.

4.3.2 Comparison of Mean Scores between Different Semantic Types

Mean score of each group in four semantic types is presented in Table 4.6. It shows that all the participants performed better in T1 ([+SR][+HK]) and T4 ([−SR][−HK]) than in T2 ([−SR][+HK]) and T3 ([+SR][−HK]). The accuracy of T2 was the lowest for Natives (88.8%) and Spanish English learners (61.2%) and the accuracy of T3 was lower than other types for French English learners (74.1%) and Chinese English learners (46.8%). Furthermore, the native English speakers produced the highest accuracy in T1 ([+SR][+HK]) (93.2%), while all the other three groups produced higher accuracy in T4([−SR][−HK]) (79.7% for French, 81.4% for Spanish, and 81.9% for Chinese).

Table 4.6 Mean scores of semantic article types

Group		T1	T2	T3	T4
Native	Mean	19.58	5.33	8.25	8.33
	Std. Deviation	1.084	0.651	0.866	0.778
	Accuracy	93.2%	88.8%	91.7%	92.6%
French	Mean	15.83	4.5	6.67	7.17
	Std. Deviation	2.639	1.378	1.211	1.329
	Accuracy	75.4%	75.0%	74.1%	79.7%

Spanish	Mean	14.83	3.67	6.84	7.33
	Std. Deviation	1.722	1.211	2.062	1.336
	Accuracy	70.6%	61.2%	75%	81.4%
Chinese	Mean	12	3.21	4.21	7.37
	Std. Deviation	3.317	1.182	1.873	1.662
	Accuracy	57.1%	53.5%	46.8%	81.9%

In order to test whether significant difference existed between these four semantic types, a one-way ANOVA and a post hoc test were conducted. The statistical software SPSS 17.0 was used to test significance difference between mean scores of four semantic types of articles, and the statistical results are shown in Table 4.7.

Table 4.7 One-way ANOVA of four semantic article types

		Sum of Squares	df	Mean Square	F	Sig.
T1	Between Group	427.324	3	142.441	21.318	0.000
	Within Group	260.583	39	6.682		
	Total	687.907	42			
T2	Between Groups	35.249	3	11.750	9.821	0.000
	Within Group	46.658	39	1.196		
	Total	81.907	42			
T3	Between Groups	134.344	3	44.781	19.829	0.000
	Within Group	88.075	39	2.258		
	Total	222.419	42			

T4	Between Groups	16.687	3	5.562	2.183	0.105
	Within Group	99.360	39	2.548		
	Total	116.047	42			

As can be seen from Table 4.7, at the significance level of 0.05, the mean scores of learners with different native languages were significantly different. P values were significant (F = 21.318, p=0.000; F=9.821, p=0.000; F=19.829, p=0.000 respectively) in the first three types: referential definites ([+SR][+HK]), generics([−SR][+HK]), and referential indefinites([+SR][−HK]). However, there was no significant difference in nonreferentials ([− SR] [− HK]), with the significance value of 0. 105. A post hoc test of multiple comparisons for each semantic type was made to further analyze the difference between different groups. Tukey HSD test of multilevel comparison shows the significance levels for four groups of learners in [+SR][+HK].

Table 4.8 Tukey HSD test of multilevel comparison in [+SR][+HK]

(I) no	(J) no	Mean Difference (I-J)	Std. Error	Sig.	95% Confidence Interval	
					Lower Bound	Upper Bound
N	F	3.750*	1.292	0.030	0.28	7.22
	S	4.750*	1.292	0.004	1.28	8.22
	C	7.583*	0.953	0.000	5.03	10.14
F	N	−3.750*	1.292	0.030	−7.22	−0.28
	S	1.000	1.492	0.908	−3.00	5.00
	C	3.833*	1.210	0.015	0.59	7.08
S	N	−4.750*	1.292	0.004	−8.22	−1.28
	F	−1.000	1.492	0.908	−5.00	3.00
	C	2.833	1.210	0.106	−0.41	6.08
C	N	−7.583*	0.953	0.000	−10.14	−5.03
	F	−3.833*	1.210	0.015	−7.08	−0.59
	S	−2.833	1.210	0.106	−6.08	0.41

* The mean difference is significant at the 0.05 level.

As can be seen from Table 4.8, there were significant differences between non-native English learners and English native speakers (p=0.030, 0.004, 0.000 respectively) on the subtype of referential definite ([+SR][+HK]). There was no significant difference between Spanish and French learners (p=0.908), while there was a significant difference (p=0.015) between the mean scores of Chinese L2 learners and French L2 learners. However, no significant difference was found between the mean scores of Chinese learners and Spanish learners (p=0.106).

Table 4.9 Tukey HSD test of multilevel comparison in [−SR][+HK]

(I) no	(J) no	Mean Difference (I-J)	Std. Error	Sig.	95% Confidence Interval Lower Bound	Upper Bound
N	F	0.833	0.547	0.433	−0.63	2.30
	S	1.667*	0.547	0.021	0.20	3.13
	C	2.123*	0.403	0.000	1.04	3.21
F	N	−0.833	0.547	0.433	−2.30	0.63
	S	0.833	0.631	0.556	−0.86	2.53
	C	1.289	0.512	0.073	−0.08	2.66
S	N	−1.667*	0.547	0.021	−3.13	−0.20
	F	−0.833	0.631	0.556	−2.53	0.86
	C	0.456	0.512	0.810	−0.92	1.83
C	N	−2.123*	0.403	0.000	−3.21	−1.04
	F	−1.289	0.512	0.073	−2.66	0.08
	S	−0.456	0.512	0.810	−1.83	0.92

* The mean difference is significant at the 0.05 level.

As is shown in Table 4.9, there were significant differences between the native English speakers and Spanish and Chinese English learners in generics ([−SR][+HK]) ($p=0.021$, 0.000 respectively). There existed no significant difference ($p=0.433$) between the French learners and native English speakers; there was no significant difference ($p=0.556$) between Spanish and French learners.

Table 4.10 Tukey HSD test of multilevel comparison in [+SR][−HK]

(I) no	(J) no	Mean Difference (I-J)	Std. Error	Sig.	95% Confidence Interval	
					Lower Bound	Upper Bound
N	F	1.583	0.751	0.169	−0.43	3.60
	S	0.917	0.751	0.618	−1.10	2.93
	C	4.039*	0.554	0.000	2.55	5.53
F	N	−1.583	0.751	0.169	−3.60	0.43
	S	−0.667	0.868	0.868	−2.99	1.66
	C	2.456*	0.704	0.006	0.57	4.34
S	N	−0.917	0.751	0.618	−2.93	1.10
	F	0.667	0.868	0.868	−1.66	2.99
	C	3.123*	0.704	0.000	1.23	5.01
C	N	−4.039*	0.554	0.000	−5.53	−2.55
	F	−2.456*	0.704	0.006	−4.34	−0.57
	S	−3.123*	0.704	0.000	−5.01	−1.23

* The mean difference is significant at the 0.05 level.

As is shown in Table 4.10, there was a significant difference (p=0.000, 0.006, 0.000 respectively) in the context of referential indefinites ([+SR][−HK]) between the mean scores of Chinese L2 learners and language learners whose native languages have an article system (natives, French and Spanish English learners), that is, between the [−ART] group and the [+ART] group. However, no significant difference was found (p=0.169, 0.868, 0.618 respectively) among the language learners within the [+ART] group.

Table 4.11 Tukey HSD test of multilevel comparison in [−SR][−HK]

(I) no	(J) no	Mean Difference* (I-J)	Std. Error	Sig.	95% Confidence Interval	
					Lower Bound	Upper Bound
N	F	1.167	0.798	0.470	−0.97	3.31
	S	1.000	0.798	0.598	−1.14	3.14
	C	1.491	0.589	0.070	−0.09	3.07
F	N	−1.167	0.798	0.470	−3.31	0.97
	S	−0.167	0.922	0.998	−2.64	2.31
	C	0.325	0.747	0.972	−1.68	2.33
S	N	−1.000	0.798	0.598	−3.14	1.14
	F	0.167	0.922	0.998	−2.31	2.64
	C	0.491	0.747	0.912	−1.51	2.50
C	N	−1.491	0.589	0.070	−3.07	0.09
	F	−0.325	0.747	0.972	−2.33	1.68
	S	−0.491	0.747	0.912	−2.50	1.51

* The mean difference is significant at the 0.05 level.

As can be seen from Table 4.11, in the results of mean scores of nonreferentials, there was no significant difference ($p=0.470$, 0.598, 0.070 respectively) between native speakers and the non-native speakers. Furthermore, there existed no significant difference ($p=0.070$, 0.972, 0.912 respectively) between the [+ART] group and the [−ART] group learners.

4.4 Data Analysis

4.4.1 Difference of Accuracy with Different Native Languages

From the above results of the experiment, it was found that the performance of native English speakers was significantly better than that of the non-native speakers in the first type of referential definite ([+SR][+HK]). In generics ([−SR][+HK]), there was no significant difference between French learners and native English speakers. But there were significant differences between native speakers and the other two groups: Chinese and Spanish learners. In the third type, referential indefinite [+SR][−HK], the significant difference only existed between Chinese and Native English speakers. No significance was found between the non-native speakers and the native English speakers in the type of nonreferential([−SR][−HK]). The comparison of mean scores between Spanish learners was basically consistent with those of French learners in the comparison of four types of articles, and no significant difference was found in all the four types. The difference of accuracy between groups can be explained by different markedness across languages.

As a category of functional words, articles exist in some languages but do not exist in some other languages. This phenomenon is related to the typological differences across languages and it is particularly associated with the factors of

NPs. The NPs have different characteristics in form in different languages, which is mainly determined by three major factors: number, gender and case. This difference can also be demonstrated through the comparison of the four languages: Spanish, French, English and Chinese.

Table 4.12 Comparison of markedness among four languages

	Number	Gender	Case
Spanish	+	+	−
French	+	+	−
English	+	−	−
Chinese	−	−	−

As is shown in Table 4.12, Spanish and French are similar to English in their semantic and syntactic structure. They have similar properties to English as they both have article systems. What's more, they are more marked than English in gender and number. As can be seen from the above table, Spanish and French have the feature of gender and number: nouns can be identified both by genders (masculine, feminine or neuter) and by the number (plural or singular). English noun phrases are only morphologically marked in number and Chinese has none of the features of number, gender or case.

Different typological distributions of the above features lead to the presence and absence of articles in different languages. If the typological difference is set as a parameter of markedness to identify the differences between different languages, the parameter has two opposite features which divide the four languages into two groups: Spanish, French and English belong to the group in which nouns are morphologically distinguished by the parameter of number, and Chinese falls into the other group in which articles do not exist. What's more, the number of articles also varies due to different morphological distribution of nouns. There are six article forms in French, nine forms in Spanish, and four forms in English, while Chinese has no article system. It explains why French and Spanish English learners outperformed significantly Chinese English learners (see Table 4.13).

Table 4.13　A comparison of distribution of articles

	English		French			Spanish				Chinese		
Types of Articles	singular	plural	singular		plural	singular		plural		singular		plural
			M	F		M	F	M	F	M	F	
Definite Art.	*the*	*the*	*le*	*la*	*les*	*el*	*la*	*los*	*las*	×	×	×
Indefinite Art.	*a/an*	×	*un*	*une*	*des*	*un*	*una*	*unos*	*unas*	×	×	×
Partitive Art.	×	×	*du*	*de la*	*des*	×	×	×	×	×	×	×
Zero Art.			×	×	×	×	×	×	×	×	×	×
Neuter Art.	×	×	×	×	×	*lo*		×	×	×	×	×

To what extent does the number of articles affect the acquisition of articles? What is the relationship between the degree of markedness of articles and the acquisition of articles? Contrastive Analysis Hypothesis (CAH) claimed that the cross-linguistic difference was the main reason to lead to the learning difficulties. Wherever the differences existed, negative transfer would occur, thus interfering with the acquisition of the target langue. Eckman's (1977) Markedness Differential Hypothesis (MDH) is different from CAH. MDH holds that language transfer only happens when the target language is more marked than the native language. According to MDH, the areas of L2 which differ from L1 and are more marked than L1 will be difficult. Comparatively, those areas of L2 which are different from L1 but are not more marked than L1 will not be difficult. Meanwhile Eckman (1977) proposes that typological markedness is one of the essential factors which determines transferability. He claims (1977: 320) that "the notion of *degree of difficulty* corresponds to the notion *typologically marked*".

Applying MDH to the analysis of articles, we find it possible to explain difference of mean scores among the learners with different native languages and the relative degree of their learning difficulty. As is shown in Table 4. 13, Spanish and French articles are nearly equally marked in the distribution of articles: both have gender and number distinctions, and Spanish has an extra neuter article. English has the feature of number, but not gender. In contrast, Chinese possesses none of the two features. Thus a conclusion can be made that Spanish and French are more marked than English and Chinese is less marked than English. That well explains why the mean scores of Spanish and French English learners are 33. 17 and 34. 17, higher than the population mean of 1. 8%, and 4. 87% respectively. Chinese English learners' mean score is 26. 26, significantly lower than the overall average of 19. 39%. The post hoc test was in line with mean scores: there was significant difference between native speakers and non-native speakers, but the degree was different.

The difference shows that Chinese speakers have greater difficulty with English articles than Spanish and French speakers. That was in accordance with Eckman's hypothesis: when an aspect of the target language is more marked than the native language, the negative transfer of native language will arise, thus contributing to the learning difficulty; when the target language is less marked than the native language, transfer will not happen and language learners will not encounter the learning difficulty.

The differences between Spanish and French L2 learners whose native languages have an article system and Chinese L2 learners whose native language has no article system is consistent with Master's (1988) findings. He (1988) made a pseudolongitudinal study and analyzed cross-linguistic interlanguage of articles. The participants in this study were 20 L2 English learners with five different native languages. They were divided into two groups: the [+ART] group including German and Spanish speakers and the [−ART] group including Chinese, Japanese and Russian speakers. Each group was measured and analyzed based on different language proficiency of the learners: the basilang (BA), low-mesolang (LM), mid-mesolang (MM) and high-mesolang (HM). Through the comparison of the two groups, Master made a conclusion that "the subjects whose first language contained an article system differed markedly in English article acquisition from those whose first language did not contain such a system, showing that the usage of English article, especially at the beginning levels, is clearly influenced by the first language" (Master, 1988: 3).

4.4.2 Difference of Accuracy in Different Semantic Types

The difference of accuracy produced by the participants was demonstrated to be closely related not only with different native language backgrounds but also with different semantic types. The experimental results in Table 4.6 show that all the participants produced higher accuracy in T1([+SR][+HK]) and T4([−SR][−HK]) and higher error rate in T2([−SR][+HK]) and T3([+SR][−HK]). To further analyze the performance of each group, the performance of four groups in each semantic subtype was shown in Figure 4.1.

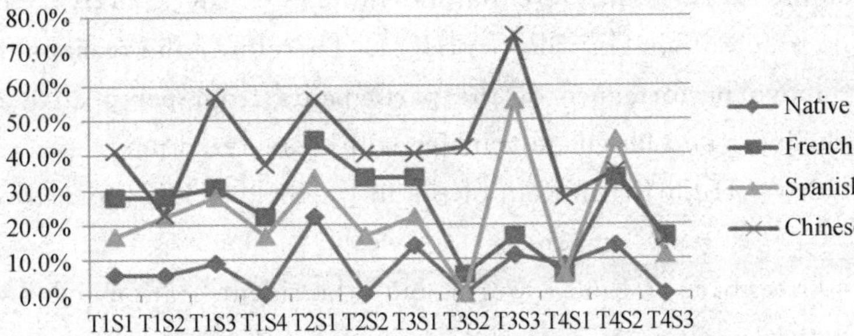

Figure 4.1 The error rate of each subtype

As the graph in Figure 4.1 shows, the error rate of twelve subtypes differed among the learners with different native languages. The native English speakers exhibited the lowest error rate, while Chinese English learners produced the highest except two subtypes: T1S2 and T4S2. Spanish and French learners performed better than Chinese learners but not as well as the native speakers. Of all the twelve subtypes, the error rates of T3S3 and T2S1 reached 39.5% and 39% and were the highest among all the participants. Unexpectedly, the accuracy of Spanish-speaking learners was as low as that of Chinese English learners in the score of T3S3, despite the presence of articles in Spanish. The error rate of Chinese-speaking learners reached 74.5%, the Spanish-speaking learners 55.6%, more than 50 percent. T4S1 and T4S3 enjoyed the lowest error rate and the mean error rate were 11.7% and 10.9%, respectively.

The high error rates in T3S3 and T2S1 concern the usage of the definite article *the* in generics ([−SR][+HK]) and the indefinite article *an* in referential indefinites ([+SR][−HK]). The high accuracy of T4S1 and T4S3 relates to the usage of indefinite articles in referential indefinites ([+SR][−HK]) and in nonreferentials ([−SR][−HK]). Therefore, the reasons for the above performance of the participants from perspective of markedness and language transfer will be analyzed next.

4.4.2.1 High Error Rate of *the* in [−SR][+HK] and *an* in [+SR][−HK]

Greenberg (1966) sorts out the identification of two structural entities of "marked" and "unmarked" that present a consistently asymmetric relationship with respect to distribution of syntagmatic structure and paradigmatic complexity. The entity that is consistently more widely distributed or simpler in form is called "unmarked", and its opposite entity is called "marked". An important concept of markedness which must be pointed out is that "markedness relations are not fixed, but rather depend on the language-internal evaluation of the terms of an opposition" (Battistella, 1990: 4). That is to say, a marked form as opposed to a different form within a language might be an unmarked one as opposed to a third form or a marked form in one language can be unmarked in another.

French and Spanish both have an article system and the structure of these two languages seems to be more marked than English. However, there exist differences in some particular instances. In the expression of generic reference, for example, Spanish and French consistently and systematically use the definite articles to mark an entire class or a noun in an abstract, general, or universal sense; in contrast, such a generic reference seldom appears in English. For instance, in the following sentences:

1. (a) Dogs are intelligent. /A dog is intelligent. /The dog is intelligent.

   (b) 狗很聪明。

   (c) Le Chien est intelligent. (French)

   (d) Los perros son inteligentes. (Spanish)

2. (a) I like cats.

   (b) 我喜欢猫。

   (c) J'aime le chat. (French)

   (d) Me gustan los gatos. (Spanish)

The standard expression of generic reference is bare nouns in Chinese. There are no plural marking or determiners. We just use the noun to refer to a whole class. For instance, in 1(b) and 2(b), 狗 and 猫 are bare nouns, which are used to refer to the whole class. In English, generics can be expressed in three forms: definite plurals, indefinite plurals and bare plurals. However, Chinese only use bare plurals to express generic ideas. Therefore, when it was necessary to use the definite article *the* and an adjective to refer to a whole class, Chinese English learners tended to use bare nouns under the influence of native language.

It seems that definite articles in French and Spanish distinguish between masculine and feminine, singular and plural forms, thus are more marked than English. However, the uses of the definite articles in [－SR][＋HK] are different. For instance:

3. (a) He has black hair.
   (b) 他长着一头黑发。
   (c) Il a les cheveux noirs. (French)
   (d) El tiene el pelo negro. (Spanish)
4. (a) I am studying music.
   (b) 我在学习音乐。
   (c) J'etudie la musique. (French)
   (d) Estudio la musica. (Spanish)

In the above sentences, the definite articles are needed in French and Spanish to refer to the generic reference regardless of countability. However, the zero article needs to be used in English when the referent of an NP is uncountable. French and Spanish L2 learners tended to use the definite article to refer to the generic reference due to negative transfer of their native language. According to Givon's (1990) criteria of Markedness Theory, the structure in Chinese, French and Spanish tends to be less complex than that in English in [－SR][＋HK]. Therefore, the generics in Chinese, French and Spanish are less marked than those in English with respect to structural complexity, frequency distribution and cognitive complexity. According to the first prediction of Eckman's (1977: 321)

MDH, "those areas of the target language which differ from the native language and are more marked than the native language will be difficult". That explains the lowest accuracy of the definite article in [−SR][+HK].

The experimental result is in accordance with the findings of Ionin (2010). He also explored transfer of native language in article acquisition with generic interpretation of plural NPs. He made a comparison between L1 Spanish learners whose first language has articles and Korean English learners whose native language does not contain articles. He proposed a hypothesis that the Spanish-speaking learners of English would transfer the definite plurals from their native language to English in the generic interpretation of NPs. The aim of his experiment was to investigate whether language transfer would happen and whether the recovery from language transfer was possible in the structure of interpretation of plural noun phrases. His study consisted of two tasks: an acceptability judgment task to test the learners' familiarity and proficiency of English articles and a truth value judgment task to examine the participants' ability to correctly interpret English plurals as generic versus specific. Two experiments were conducted in the research: the former was conducted among the EFL learners and the latter among the ESL learners to distinguish the different language proficiency of the participants. Through a series of experimental analyses, including ANOVA, T-test and analysis of covariance, Ionin concluded that language transfer existed in the interpretation of language learners when they acquired the generic interpretation of English articles. At the same time, Ionin also found that with improved proficiency and increased acquisition of the target language, Spanish L2 learners performed as well as Korean L2 learners on the understanding of definite plurals. It proved that recovery from first language transfer was possible. The experimental results provided support for his hypothesis: Spanish L2 learners overaccepted the generic interpretation of English definite plurals to a greater extent than their counterparts of Korean L2 learners whose native language is an articleless language.

As to the high error rate of the indefinite article *an*, it can be explained by the effect of negative transfer of L2 language learners caused by different degree of markedness. In English, the function of *a/an* is similar to the numeral *yi* (one) in Chinese. However, *an* can only be used in a limited syntactic context in English, i. e., the word must begin with a vowel. Therefore, the indefinite article *an* is more marked than the numeral *yi* in Chinese. The indefinite articles *un/une* in French and *un/ una* in Spanish have the distinction of gender as well as number which seem to be more marked than the indefinite articles in English. However, the standard of the distinction in French and Spanish is different from that of *an* in English. The feature of *a/an* is more marked than *un/une* in French and *un/una* in Spanish within the constraint of pronunciation, while the indefinite articles in French and Spanish are more marked than those in English in terms of gender. According to the second prediction of Eckman's (1977: 321) MDH, "the relative degree of difficulty of the areas of the target language which are more marked than the native language will correspond to the relative degree of the markedness". The markedness degree is comparatively more difficult in the usage of *an*, which predicts more difficulty to acquire the specific usage of *an*. Therefore, it is of no difficulty to understand the high error rate of *an* in T3S3.

4.4.2.2 High Accuracy of *the* in [+SR][+HK] and *a* in [−SR][−HK]

Of the twelve subtypes, T4S1, T4S3 and T3S2 had the lowest error rates (11.7%, 10.9%, and 11.9%). The results were in accord with the results of one-way ANOVA. All the participants, no matter whether their native languages have article system, achieved high scores in T4S1 (equative noun phrases), T4S3 (indefinite article to refer to price, speed, ratio etc., meaning "every", "per") and T3S2 (first mention of the [+SR] NP which is assumed not known to the hearer). Besides, the error rates of T1S2 (referent previously mentioned in the discourse) and T1S4 (referent physically present) were also low, 19.6% and 19.0% respectively.

The definite article *the* in T1S4, referent physically present, is similar to the demonstrative *nei* (that) in Chinese and the indefinite article in T3S2 is similar to the numeral *yi* (one) in Chinese. Li and Thompson (1981: 131) pointed out when making comparative analysis between English and Chinese grammar in their book *Mandarin Chinese: A Reference Grammar* that although Mandarin Chinese has no equivalents of the English articles, "the demonstrative *nei* (that)... is beginning to function as *the* if it is not stressed and the numeral *yi* (one), if not stressed, is beginning to function as *a*". For example, in T1S4, (________ *man standing over there is the very man that we have been talking about*), the definite article in the phrase *the man standing over there* can find its equivalents in the other three languages:

5. (a) the man standing over there
   (b) 那边站着的那个人
   (c) la personne qui reste debout la-bas(French)
   (d) el persona que esta alla de pie(Spanish)

In this example, the definite article *the* in English, *la* in French, *el* in Spanish and the demonstrative *nei* with the classifier *ge* (that) in Chinese perform a similar function. That accounts for why Chinese English learners had better performance in T3S2 and T1S4 than their performance in other subtypes. The corresponding functions of the numerals and demonstratives between learners' native languages and the target language will be further analyzed in Chapter 5.

The uses of articles in [+SR][-HK] and [-SR][-HK] can also find their corresponding features in French and Spanish. The usage of *the* in T1S2 and T1S4 is similar to the usage of the definite article *le*/*la*/*les* in French and *el*/*la*/*los*/*las* in Spanish. The usage of indefinite article *a* in T4S1, T4S3 and T3S2 is similar to the uses of indefinite articles *un*/*une*/*des* in French and *un*/*una*/*unos*/*unas* in Spanish. The uses have different forms based on gender and number in Spanish and French. The features of definite and indefinite articles in French and Spanish are more marked than *the* and *a* in English, which explains the better performance of French and Spanish learners in the above mentioned subtypes. As for the high error rate of the indefinite article *an*, it is mainly caused by the fact that different standard of distinction leads to different markedness as mentioned above.

4.5 Discussion

The experiment in this chapter examines the forms and uses of articles in English learners' productions. The aim of this experiment is to investigate how language transfer and markedness function to cause differences between language learners with different native languages.

At the beginning of the experiment, three research questions were raised. The first question concerns whether language learners' native language will affect their performance. It was found that there existed significant difference between French and Spanish English learners whose native languages have an article system and Chinese English learners whose native language has no article system. French and Spanish L2 learners had significantly outperformed Chinese L2 learners. This finding demonstrates that Chinese speakers have greater difficulty to acquire English articles than Spanish and French speakers. No significant difference was found between Spanish and French learners' mean scores in all four types. In other words, there existed significant difference between the mean score of the [+ART] and [−ART] group L2 learners, but there existed no significant difference between the means cores within [+ART] group L2 learners in this experiment. The experimental results offer an affirmative response to the first research question, confirming the hypothesis that language learners' native language will affect their performance in article acquisition. The findings suggest that whether language learners' native language has an article system will influence their performance. When a structure of the native language is unmarked and the target language is marked, the negative transfer of native language will arise. It contributes to the learning difficulty of language learners. On the contrary, negative transfer will not happen and language learners will not encounter the learning difficulty if the native language is more marked than the target language.

It must be pointed out that French and Spanish learners failed to acquire English articles as target-like as native speakers, although French and Spanish contain article system and the usage of articles in French and Spanish seems to be more marked in number and gender. Significant difference was found between native speakers and non-native speakers, including French and Spanish. Two factors are considered to contribute to this result. First, language input of French and Spanish learners was not enough. The participants in this experiment were not English majors and they had studied in UCLan for less than a year when the experiment was conducted. Second, the usage of articles in French and Spanish are not always more marked than in English. As is mentioned above, the definite articles are used before nouns to refer to generic reference in French and Spanish. In contrast, all forms of articles can be used in generics in English. The use of generics in French and Spanish is less marked than in English with respect to structural complexity, frequency distribution and cognitive complexity. French and Spanish learners tended to transfer unmarked forms in their native languages to the target language and use the definite article in generics. Therefore, the significant difference between French and Spanish English learners and native speakers within [+ART] group is not the denial of markedness and language transfer.

The second research question asks whether there exists difference between groups of language learners in different semantic types of articles. Mean scores of four groups in different semantic types of articles were compared. It exhibited significant difference between native English speakers and Chinese L2 learners in the first three types. No significant difference was found between them in T4, but the P-value was only slightly higher than 0.05. The mean scores of native English speakers and [+ART] group L2 learners were significantly different in T1. No significant difference was found in T4 between native English speakers and all L2 English learners. Moreover, the participants all performed better in T1 and T4, and the accuracy of T2 and T3 were comparatively low. Better performance of L2 English learners in T1 and T4 mainly resulted from language transfer. Chinese learners tended to transfer the usage of the numeral *yi* (one), demonstratives *zhe* (this), *na* (that) in their native language to the target language. Articles in French and Spanish are more marked than English, which contributes to less difficulty for them to acquire English articles. The facts that French and Spanish learners achieved high accuracy and there existed significant difference between the mean score of native English speakers and [+ART] group L2 learners seem to be contradictory. It may be caused by overuse of the definite article by French and Spanish learners, which will be investigated in the next chapter.

The third question relates to when language transfer happens in article acquisition. The answer to the third question is that the occurrence of language transfer depends on the degree of markedness. It is widely accepted that language transfer plays an essential part in SLA. Ionin (2006) claimed that three factors contributed to the acquisition of English articles in SLA: L1 transfer, language input and Universal Grammar. The experimental results in this chapter also supported that language transfer functioned in article acquisition of L2 learners. As for when language transfer happens due to markedness in article acquisition, it depends on the markedness degree. The significant difference between [+ART] group learners and [−ART] group learners and the high error rate of *the* in the semantic type of [−SR][+HK] demonstrates that when the target language is different from and more marked than native language, it will be more difficult to acquire. Therefore, an unmarked form in native language will be transferred to the target language in which the corresponding structure is more marked in the process of article acquisition.

This finding is consistent with the findings of James (1998), Liao (1998) and Zobl(1984). James found that British learners tended to add subjects when learning Portuguese which was not grammatical in Portuguese. He explained it from the perspective of markedness and claimed that the British learners transferred the unmarked forms in their native language in the process of acquisition. English is a subject-prominent language and Portuguese a null-subject language. According to Givon's (1990) criteria of markedness, subject-prominent languages are unmarked whereas null-subject languages are marked. Therefore, Portuguese is more marked than English in terms of subject. According to the prediction of Eckman's (1977) MDH, the relative unmarked subject form will be transferred to the target language. James suggested that it explained why British learners encountered difficulty in learning Portuguese. In a similar study, Liao (1998) examined the difficulty for the English-speaking learners to acquire the Chinese sentence structure. As Chinese sentence structure is featured by OSV, which is more marked than the English SVO structure, the English-speaking learners transferred the unmarked form in their native language into the target language. Zobl also claims that language learners tend to transfer the unmarked forms rather than the marked ones on account of the avoidance of using marked forms. Zobl (1980a, 1980b, 1982, 1983 and 1984) made a series of studies to investigate markedness from typological perspective. He offered three senses in which rules could be marked: "The first is typological specialization. The second is that the structural properties of a language may be marked as a result of typological inconsistency. The third is that typologically indeterminacy occurs when a structure predicted on the basis of a language's overall typology is not found" (cited in Ellis, 1999: 320). He compared English interrogative "how many" with its French equivalent "combien":

6. (a) Combien d'oranges voulez-vous? (French)
(b) Combien voulez-vous d'organges? (French)
(c) How many oranges do you want?
* (d) How many do you want oranges?

(Zobl, 1984:86)

6(a) and 6(b) are both grammatically correct in French. In other words, extraction is permitted in French. English follows the universal tendency and avoids the non-extraction. Therefore, 6(d) is not permitted in English. Zobl suggested when the corresponding structure in target language was unmarked learners resisted transferring the marked forms in their native language.

The findings in the present study have answered the questions proposed at the beginning of this chapter. The performance of L2 English learners will be influenced by their different native languages. They will transfer corresponding or similar structures in their native languages to the target language in article acquisition. As for when language transfer happens, it depends on cross-linguistic comparison of markedness degree.

Chapter 5 Experiment 2: The Blank-filling Task

Quirk (1972: 676) stated that "the use of articles is not the only possibility for 'determining' nouns: the/a/no/what/this/every/each/other pen. These words and some others are called determiners. They form a set of closed-system items that are mutually exclusive with each other". Articles are a kind of determiners and other determiners also appear in positions where the articles are used to serve the same functions. Therefore, they should also be involved in a comprehensive analysis of articles. Consequently, the qualitative and quantitative analyses of determiners other than articles are conducted in this chapter. A blank-filling task (see Appendix B) is employed, and the same participants in Experiment 1 participated in this experiment.

5.1 Research Questions

The previous experiment investigates the differences between different groups of learners as well as the differences between groups of language learners in different semantic types of articles. It also explores when language transfer happens due to different degrees of markedness in article acquisition. What caused the differences between different groups and does there exist overuse or underuse in article acquisition? Will the acquisition of these determiners affect the acquisition of articles since some determiners also play similar functions in place of articles? Therefore, the experiment in this chapter attempts to explore the answers to the following three questions:

(1) Do differences exist in accuracy of articles and other determiners between different semantic types?

(2) Does overuse or underuse of articles exist among the learners with different native languages?

(3) How does language transfer happen due to different degree of markedness in article acquisition among [+ART] group L2 learners and [−ART] group L2 learners?

5.2 Research Method

5.2.1 Participants

The participants in this experiment are the same as those in the first one: 43 students majoring in Finance in University of Central Lancashire (UCLan) in the UK. The participants were divided into 4 groups according to their native languages.

5.2.2 Instrument

This experiment consists of both quantitative and qualitative analyses. Corpus-based approach is used in this experiment. With advanced computer technology, corpus linguistics, as a new methodology, studies naturally-occurring language use. According to Biber et al. (2000), corpus-based approach has four features which are also marked as the advantages of it:

> It is empirical, analyzing the actual patterns of use in natural texts.
> It utilizes a large and principled collection of natural texts, known as a "corpus", as the basis for analysis.
> It makes extensive use of computers for analysis, using both automatic and interactive techniques.
> It depends on both quantitative and qualitative analytical techniques.
> (Biber et al., 2000: 4)

The present experiment makes use of the corpus-based approach to analyze the frequencies of the different types of articles and to identify whether there exist differences between different corpora with different native languages.

5.2.3 Classification of Determiners

With articles belonging to a kind of determiners, other determiner are also involved in the present study. Determiners precede the pre-modifying adjectives in NPs and denote such referential meanings as specific reference, generic reference, definite quantity or indefinite quantity. J. Aarts and F. Aarts (1988: 125) stated that "the function determiner can be realized by a wide range of items such as the definite article, the indefinite article, possessive pronouns, demonstrative pronouns, numerals etc. These items occur in a fixed order with respect to each other". Therefore the determiners can be classified into different types according to different standards. In terms of positions, determiners fall into three categories: pre-determiner, central-determiner and post-determiner; in terms of semantic functions, determiners usually fall into two types: quantifying determiners and referential determiners. The former type focuses on the indefiniteness of the NPs while the latter centers on the referential functions, including articles, demonstrative determiners, possessive determiners, genitive case, and relative determiners. The classification of determiners in this experiment focuses on the referentiality of the determiners and also employs Huebner's four semantic types. The semantic classification of determiners is presented in Table 5.1.

Table 5.1 The semantic classification of determiners

Semantic Types	Determiners
Type 1: referential definites ([+SR][+HK])	1. possessives (my, your, his, her, our...) 2. genitives (John's, my friend's...) 3. demonstratives (this, that, these, those) 4. the definite article 5. the zero article before proper nouns
Type 2: generics ([−SR][+HK])	articles

Type 3: referential indefinites ([+SR][−HK])	1. universal quantifiers (all, every, any, each) 2. indefinite determiners (a/an, no, some, many, much, a few, a little...)
Type 4: nonreferentials ([−SR][−HK])	indefinite determiners

As is shown in Table 5. 1, the determiners fall into four types, based on their referential meanings: referential definites, generics, referential indefinites and nonreferentials. The accuracy and differences between different groups are analyzed according to the semantic types of the determiners.

5.2.4 Procedure

The participants were required to complete a passage by filling in the blanks with proper determiners where needed. The passage was chosen from the National College Entrance Examination (NCEE). The content of the passage is about the study of power of pets in life. It contains 295 words and 59 blanks, including 45 articles and 14 other determiners. As is shown in table 5. 1, the determiners in the 59 blanks fall into four semantic types: referential definites, generics, referential indefinites and nonreferentials, among which 15 in Type 1, 24 in Type 2, 11 in Type 3, and 9 in Type 4. After the completion of the blank-filling task, the researcher converted the passages to plain text files, and created four mini-corpora: the corpus of native English speakers, Chinese English learners, French English learners, and that of Spanish English learners. After text edition and collation, the researcher made use of the software of MicroConcord to finish the text retrieval and analysis. It aims to explore the accuracy and usage of articles and other determiners in separate corpora.

Since no significance was found between the French group and the Spanish group in each semantic type in Experiment 1, and both of their native languages have an article system, the researcher first analyzes the two corpora of French and Spanish learners to find whether there is significant difference in each semantic type of articles and other type of determiners. If no significant difference exists between these two corpora, they will be combined into one to make it convenient to analyze.

Statistical analyses are made in frequency of correct answers and comparison of different semantic types to further explore whether there exists overuse or underuse in determiners. All the statistics are analyzed by using SPSS 17.0 and P values of 0.5 or lower are considered to be statistically significant.

5.3 Results

First, the researcher established the corpora of Spanish and French L2 learners for the analysis of the difference within the [+ART] group learners. The research hypothesis is that there is no significant difference between the corpora of Spanish and French learners. The chi-square test shows that there existed no significant difference between the two corpora of articles and other determiners in frequency ($X^2 = 0.470$, $p = 0.493$ and

$X^2=0.929$, p=0.335 respectively) (see Table 5.2).

Table 5.2 Chi-square test of frequency between the corpora of Spanish and French learners

Word	Freq in Corpus F	Freq in Corpus S	Chi-square	Significance(p)
the	62	74	1.104	0.293
a	50	50	0.000	0.998
an	19	17	0.111	0.739
Zero article	105	109	0.081	0.775
Total articles	236	250	0.470	0.493
Other determiners	118	104	0.929	0.335

Furthermore, no significant difference was found between the two corpora in terms of each subtype of the article system (definite, indefinite and zero article). It indicates that the performance of French and Spanish language learners was similar in the usage of articles. It is in accordance with the results of Experiment 1, that is, there was no significant difference between the mean scores of French and Spanish learners in each of the four types ([+SR][+HK], p=0.908; [−SR][+HK], p=0.556; [+SR][−HK], p=0.868; [−SR][−HK], p=0.998 respectively). Therefore, the two corpora were merged into one corpus of L2 learners whose native languages contain article system to facilitate the analysis.

Therefore, difference in accuracy and four semantic types of three corpora are made: Corpus 1 (native English speakers), Corpus 2 (French and Spanish English learners), and Corpus 3 (Chinese English learners).

5. 3. 1 Difference in Accuracy of Determiners between Different Groups

Table 5. 3 presents the accuracy of articles and other determiners of the learners with different native languages. Through the general comparison of accuracy, we can have an overall picture of the learners' usage of determiners.

Table 5. 3 Accuracy of determiners among different groups

		Corpus 1	Corpus 2	Corpus 3	Total
Definite article	Correct	55	36	55	146
	Total	60	60	95	215
	Percentage	91. 66%	60%	57. 89%	67. 9%
Indefinite article	Correct	154	124	127	405
	Total	204	204	323	731
	Percentage	75. 49%	60. 78%	39. 31%	55. 4%
Zero article	Correct	176	152	243	571
	Total	276	276	437	989
	Percentage	63. 76%	55. 07%	55. 6%	57. 73%
Other determiners	Correct	59	37	31	127
	Total	168	168	266	602
	Percentage	35. 11%	22. 02%	11. 65%	21. 09%

The figures in Table 5. 3 show the overall performance of learners with different native languages. In terms of the performance of students with different native languages, the native English speakers outperformed the L2 learners significantly in each type. The accuracy of French and Spanish learners took the second place and the accuracy of Chinese learners was the lowest, i.e., the performance of the [+ART] group was significantly better than the [−ART] group. As for different types of articles, the accuracy of the definite article was the highest, 91.66% for native English speakers, 60% for the Spanish and French learners and 57% for Chinese learners respectively. The accuracy of other determiners is the lowest (35.11% for native English speakers, 22.02% for Spanish and French L2 learners, and 11.65% for Chinese learners respectively).

In order to investigate whether there existed significant differences of the frequencies of determiners between different groups, the researcher used the software of SPSS 17.0 to perform further statistical analysis. Table 5.4 reports the comparison of frequency of determiners between the corpus of French and Spanish learners and the corpus of Chinese learners.

Table 5.4 Chi-square test of frequency between Corpus 2 and Corpus 3

Word	Freq in Corpus 3	Freq in Corpus 2	Chi-square	Significance(p)
the	323	136	17.063	0.000***
Indefinite articles	169	136	4.434	0.035*
Zero article	383	214	2.343	0.126
Total articles	875	486	6.368	0.012*
Other determiners	246	222	15.405	0.000***

Note: The asterisks(*) indicate significance level.

As the results in Table 5.4 reveal, there existed significant difference between the corpus of Chinese learners and Spanish and French language learners in frequency of articles ($X^2=6.368$, $p=0.012$). There was significant difference in frequencies of the definite article, indefinite articles and other determiners ($X^2=17.063$, $p=0.000$; $X^2=4.434$, $p=0.035$; $X^2=15.405$, $p=0.000$ respectively). However, of all kinds of articles, the frequency of the zero article revealed no significant difference between the two corpora ($X^2=2.343$, $p=0.126$).

Table 5.5 Chi-square test of frequency between Corpus 1 and Corpus 3

Word	Freq in Corpus 3	Freq in Corpus 1	Chi-square	Significance(p)
the	323	137	15.809	0.000***
Indefinite articles	169	204	42.376	0.000***
Zero article	383	222	0.982	0.322
Total articles	875	563	0.219	0.639
Other determiners	246	145	0.392	0.531

Table 5.5 shows the comparison of frequency in article system between the corpus of Chinese learners and that of the native English speakers. There was a significant difference between the two corpora in the frequency of the definite article and indefinite articles ($X^2=15.809$, $p=0.000$; $X^2=42.376$, $p=0.000$ respectively). As for the zero article and other determiners, there existed no significant differences ($X^2=0.982$, $p=0.322$; $X^2=0.392$, $p=0.531$ respectively). Moreover, there was no significant difference in the overall frequency of articles ($X^2=0.219$, $p=0.639$).

Table 5.6 Chi-square test of frequency between Corpus 1 and Corpus 2

Word	Freq in Corpus 2	Freq in Corpus 1	Chi-square	Significance(p)
the	136	137	0.019	0.892
Indefinite articles	136	204	14.869	0.000***
Zero article	214	222	0.240	0.624
Total articles	486	563	7.362	0.007**
Other determiners	222	145	16.258	0.000***

Table 5.6 shows the comparison of accuracy in articles between the corpus of Spanish and French L2 learners and that of the native English speakers. The frequency of [+ART] L2 learners group was significantly different from the group of native English speakers in the overall frequency of articles ($X^2 = 7.362$, $p = 0.007$). There was significant difference in the frequency of the indefinite articles ($X^2 = 14.869$, $p = 0.000$). No significant difference in frequency of the definite article, and the zero article ($X^2 = 0.019$, $p = 0.892$ and $X^2 = 0.240$, $p = 0.624$ respectively) was detected between the two groups. In addition, there was significant difference in frequency of other determiners ($X^2 = 16.258$, $p = 0.000$).

5.3.2 Difference in Accuracy of Determiners between Different Semantic Types

Table 5.7 reveals the accuracy of the articles as well as other determiners in each semantic type among learners with different native languages. It offers a clear view of which article was used for each type as well as which type of articles the learners had acquired most successfully.

Table 5.7 Accuracy between different semantic types with different native languages

		Type 1 [+SR][+HK]	Type 2 [−SR][+HK]	Type 3 [+SR][−HK]	Type 4 [−SR][−HK]
Chinese	Correct	191	109	104	18
	Total	443	285	323	38
	Percentage	43.1%	38.2%	32.2%	47.4%
F&S	Correct	128	87	76	23
	Total	300	180	204	24
	Percentage	42.6%	48.3%	37.2%	95.8%
Native	Correct	245	114	105	24
	Total	300	180	204	24
	Percentage	81.6%	63.3%	51.4%	100%

A conclusion can be made according to Table 5.7 that the native English speakers outperformed the other two groups in each semantic type. [+ART] L2 learners group took the second place and the performance of Chinese learners ranked the lowest except in Type 1. The order of performance on different semantic types among native English speakers and Chinese learners was the same, namely Type 4 > Type 1 > Type 2 > Type 3, while [+ART] L2 learners group had a different order: Type 4 > Type 2 > Type 1 > Type 3. French and Spanish have an article system, while Chinese has no article system. However, Chinese learners had the same order in accuracy with native English speakers while French and Spanish learners did not. In order to explore the specific reason for the difference, the researcher made a detailed presentation of the accuracy of different semantic types for learners of each group.

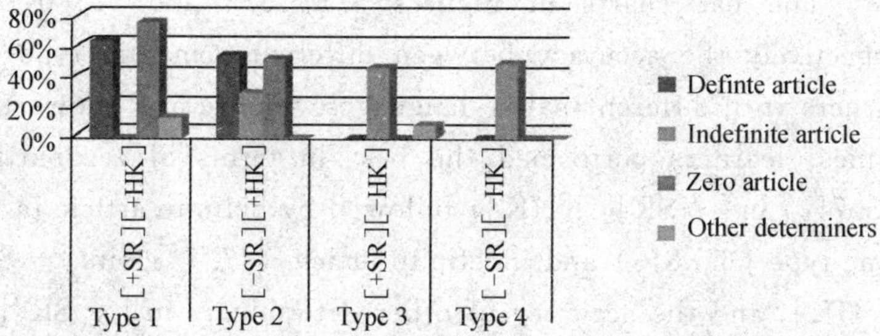

Figure 5.1 Accuracy of different semantic types of Chinese learners

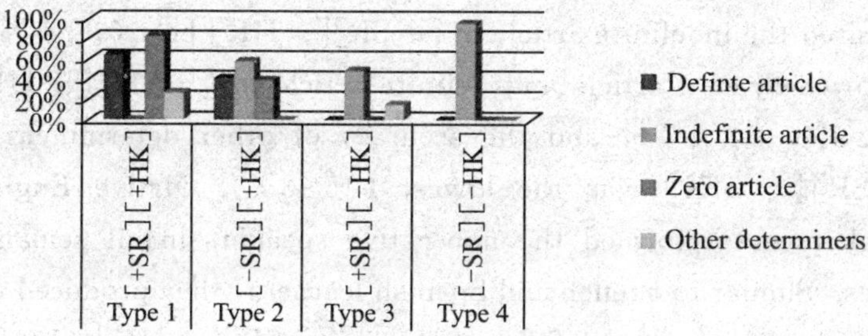

Figure 5.2 Accuracy of different semantic types of French and Spanish learners

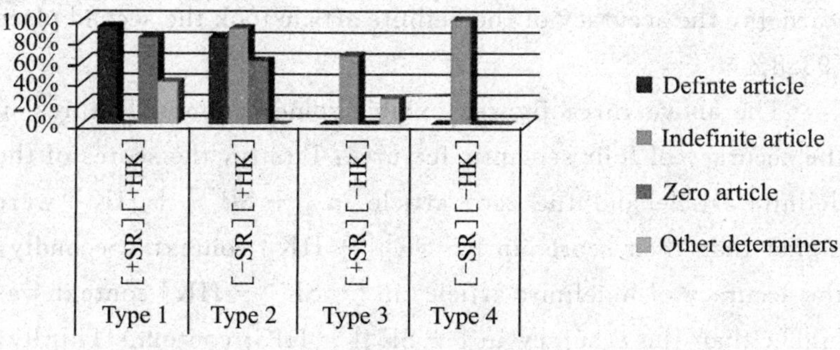

Figure 5.3 Accuracy of different semantic types of native English speakers

The bar charts in Figures 5.1, 5.2 and 5.3 report respectively the accuracy between different semantic types of learners with different native languages. Figure 5.1 shows that Chinese learners performed the best in terms of zero article (73.7%) in [+SR][+HK], followed by definite article in the same type (61.8%) and indefinite article (47.7%) in [−SR][−HK], and the accuracy of other determiners in [+SR][−HK] was the lowest (8.8%). Figure 5.2 shows the performance of French and Spanish learners in different semantic types. They acquired the indefinite article in [−SR][−HK] best (95.8 %), followed by zero article and definite article in [+SR][+HK] (83.3%, 64.4%), and the accuracy of other determiners in [+SR][− HK] was the lowest (15.3%). Native English speakers outperformed the non-native speakers in all semantic types. Similar to French and Spanish learners, they produced the highest accuracy of indefinite article in [−SR][−HK] (100%) and the lowest accuracy of other determiners in [+SR][−HK] (25%). Different from the performance of French and Spanish learners, the accuracy of the definite article took the second place (93.8%).

The above three figures exhibit some common features in the accuracy of four semantic features: Firstly, the scores of the definite article and the zero article in [+SR][+HK] were higher than their scores in [−SR][+HK] context. Secondly, the accuracy of indefinite articles in [−SR][−HK] context was higher than the accuracy in [+SR][−HK] context. Thirdly, the accuracy rate of the other determiners was very low, including native speakers and non-native speakers. However, the accuracy of the other determiners in [+SR][+HK] was higher than that in [+SR][−HK].

5.3.3 Overuse and Underuse of Articles and Other Determiners

Parrish (1987: 372) stated that "what is required to determine the rate of accuracy in Standard English is of the number of times an article should have been supplied and the number of times it was actually supplied". The researcher accordingly made a comparison between the frequency of each corpus and the frequency of the correct answers in order to investigate whether there was overuse or underuse in the use of articles with different groups of learners. SPSS 17.0 was used to test overuse and underuse of articles and other determiners.

Table 5.8 Underuse or overuse for learners with different native languages①

		Chi-square	Sig.	overuse/underuse
C	Definite	128.794	0.000***	+
	Indefinite	39.939	0.000***	−
	Zero	3.813	0.051	−
	Other determiners	2.995	0.084	−

① This table is for comparing word frequencies in corpora. The asterisks (*) indicate significance level, and the "+" and "−" signs on the right side indicate "overuse" and "underuse". Preloaded data, if any, have been taken from Rayson, Leech & Hodges (1997).

F&S	Definite	30.239	0.000***	+
	Indefinite	9.986	0.002**	−
	Zero	8.376	0.004**	−
	Other determiners	4.630	0.031*	+
N	Definite	30.893	0.000***	+
	Indefinite	0.384	0.536	+
	Zero	6.264	0.012*	−
	Other determiners	10.829	0.001*	+

The results of the chi-square test in Table 5.8 shows that significant differences were found in all three groups when comparing with the correct answers in the usage of definite article ($X^2=128.794$, $p=0.000$; $X^2=30.239$ $p=0.000$; $X^2=30.893$, $p=0.000$). Moreover, there was a phenomenon of overuse in the use of the definite article, especially for Chinese learners, with the chi-square value of 128.794. The chi-square value of group of native English speakers and that of [+ART] L2 learners group were 30.893 and 30.239 respectively, which were apparently lower than that of the Chinese learners. Furthermore, there existed underuse in the frequency of the indefinite article for Chinese learners and [+ART] L2 learners, ($X^2=39.939$, $p=0.000$; $X^2=9.986$, $p=0.002$ respectively); but there was no significant difference between the frequency generated by the native English speakers and the correct answers ($X^2=0.384$, $p=0.536$). However, Chinese learners showed no significant difference from the correct answer ($p=0.051$ and $p=0.084$ respectively) in terms of the zero article and other determiners but the [+ART] L2 learners group and the group of native English speakers reported significant differences ($p=0.004$, $p=0.012$; $p=0.031$ and $p=0.001$ respectively).

5.4 Data Analysis

As was mentioned at the beginning of this chapter, other determiners such as demonstratives, possessives can also exert similar semantic functions in the position of articles for NPs and DPs. Therefore the cross-linguistic analyses of NPs and DPs between the learners' native language and the target language are made below based on the experimental results. The analyses are made from three perspectives: difference in accuracy with different native languages, difference in accuracy with different semantic types as well as the overuse and underuse of articles and other determiners.

5.4.1 Difference in Accuracy of Determiners with Different Native Languages

Through the comparison of the different accuracy with different native languages in 5.3.1, it was found that the native English speakers had the best performance in each type of article and the accuracy of Chinese learners was the lowest. There was a significant difference between the corpus of Chinese learners and that of the native English speakers in the frequency of the definite article and indefinite article. There existed no significant differences in terms of the zero article and other determiners. As for the comparison between the corpus of Spanish and French L2 learners and that of the native English speakers, the frequency of [+ART] L2 learners group was significantly different from the group of native English speakers in the frequency of the indefinite article and no significant difference was found in the frequency of the definite article, the zero article and other determiners. The comparison of determiners between the participants' native languages and the target language is made to explain the experimental results.

5.4.1.1 Determiners in Chinese VS Determiners in English

The determiners in Chinese and English share many similarities in both syntactic and semantic aspects. Generally speaking, most determiners in Chinese can find their equivalents in English. For instance, the possessive pronoun determiners: 我的(my),你的(your),他的(his),她的(her),我们的(our),你们的(your),他们的/她们的(their),它的(its); indefinite determiners: 没有(no),一些(some),每一个(each),几个(several),很多(many),一些(a few,a little),etc.; and demonstrative determiners: 这个(this),那个(that),这些(these),那些(those),etc. However, there still exist some syntactic and semantic differences with respect to their detailed usages. Semantic differences of demonstratives and numerals between Chinese and English are analyzed here.

In Chinese, there is widespread use of determiners that can mark definiteness and specificity instead of articles. For instance, the demonstratives *zhe* (this) and *na* (that) are used to mark definiteness and specificity, and *yi* (one) is used to mark indefiniteness. Demonstratives are employed for spatial deixis by using the context of the physical surroundings of the speaker and the hearer. Definiteness is marked in Chinese by the word order of NPs or by the use of demonstratives. Both English and Chinese have a bidirectional distinction in demonstratives. Typically, one set of demonstratives (*zhe*/*zhexie* in Chinese and *this*/*these* in English) is proximal, indicating the NPs which are close to the speaker, and the other set (*na*/*naxie* in Chinese and *that*/*those* in English) is distal, indicating the NPs which are distant from the speaker. Demonstratives in English and Chinese have some similarities in syntactic and semantic features. However, there also exist some differences with respect to some particular uses. For instance, in terms of syntactic function, Chinese demonstrative *zhe* not only signifies the singular but also the plural while it is not grammatical for *this* to signify the plural in English. In terms of semantic features, both the demonstratives in English have the features of definiteness, specificity and distance. Demonstratives *this* and *that* in English express the semantic features of definiteness, distance and singular. *These* and *those* signify definiteness, distance and plural semantic features. Chinese "*zhe*" and "*na*" contain the singular and plural semantic features at the same time apart from the semantic features of definiteness and distance. Furthermore, "*zhe*" and "*na*" can also signify the semantic function of generic reference. For instance, "您这么大的老板还吃<u>这东西</u>". The demonstrative "*zhe*" (this) in this sentence indicates "*this kind of* (food)". While *this* or *these* in English does not contain the semantic denotation of generic reference. Eckman's (1977) typological markedness offers the criteria of making cross-linguistic comparison of markedness:

> A phenomenon or structure X in some language is relatively more marked than some other phenomenon or structure Y if cross-linguistically the presence of X in a language implies the presence of Y, but the presence of Y does not imply the presence of X.
>
> (Eckman, 1977: 320)

The demonstratives *zhe* and *na* in Chinese contain more semantic features than *this/that* and *these/those* in English. Chinese demonstratives can also perform both semantic functions of referential definites and generics. Therefore, they are comparatively more marked in the use of generics than English demonstratives. According to the third prediction of Eckman's MDH, "those areas of the target language which are different from the native language, but are not more marked than the native language, will not be difficult" (Eckman, 1977: 321), although the accuracy of Chinese English learners in other determiners was low (11.65%), there existed no significant difference ($p=0.531$) in accuracy between the corpus of Chinese learners and that of native English speakers in this item. What's more, it can partly explain why there existed no significant difference in the underuse of other determiners ($p=0.084$). The low accuracy, from the qualitative analysis, is found to be caused by the overuse of the definite article.

Both Chinese numeral *yi* and indefinite articles *a/an* in English signify the singular meaning in syntactic function and express indefiniteness in semantic features. Like demonstratives, there exist similarities in semantic features. However, the usage of Chinese numeral *yi* seems to exhibit obvious differences from the indefinite articles *a/an* in English with respect to markedness. For instance, *yi* can only appear before a countable noun to express the numeral meaning of *one*, a singular semantic feature of indefiniteness. It does not have the function of generic reference. While "*a/an* + NP" can also perform the semantic function of generic reference. For instance:

1. (a) A cobra is a very poisonous snake.

   *(b) 一条眼镜蛇是非常毒的蛇。

   (c) 眼镜蛇是非常毒的蛇。

1(a) is a correct sentence in English, because indefinite articles in English can be used before countable NPs to perform the semantic function of generic reference. However, it is not grammatically correct to put *yi* before the NPs to refer to generics like 1(b). In Chinese, the semantic functions of generic reference are usually performed by bare nouns. According to Eckman's (1977) typological markedness, Chinese numeral *yi* is unmarked compared with indefinite articles in English. Therefore, Chinese learners tend to transfer the unmarked form into the target language and it is of no difficulty for them to acquire indefinite articles which refer to the meaning of *per* or *every*. That explains why the accuracy of nonreferentials ([−SR][−HK]) of the Chinese English learners was the highest among four semantic types. Moreover, it is consistent with the experimental result in Experiment 1, that is, the accuracy of T4S1 and T4S3 was apparently high among Chinese learners. Chen (2004) surveyed some corpus data and claimed that "the numeral *yi* in Chinese has undergone the full process of grammaticalization, and has developed into an *a*-like indefinite article. While it is clear that *zhe* and *na* have started on the path of grammaticalization into definite articles, there is evidence which suggests that they are still far from reaching the endpoint yet"(Chen, 2004:1162).

The experimental result that Chinese transferred unmarked forms is consistent with the finding of Zobl (1984), who also investigated the transferability of native language from the perspective of markedness. He examined the contrastive structure of "*How many...*" in English and "*Combien...*" in French produced by some French learners of English. It is grammatical in French to extract the NP modified by the interrogative "*combien*" to the end of the sentence, which is not grammatical in English. Zobl claimed that the syntactic feature of extraction in French was marked and the non-extraction feature in English is unmarked. It was reported that the French learners of English tended to use the non-extraction structure, namely the unmarked form.

5.4.1.2 Determiners in French and Spanish VS Determiners in English

The determiners in French and Spanish are quite similar. They both have the features of number and gender. Like Chinese and English determiners, some usages of the determiners in French and Spanish also coincide with the determiners in English in syntactic functions and semantic features. As the comparison between Chinese and English determiners, there also exist some differences between the determiners in French, Spanish and those in English. It is known that the selection of determiners in French and Spanish depends heavily on the property of nouns,

i. e., they are closely associated with the grammatical gender of the head NPs. What does the property of NPs imply? One obvious indication is that the selected determiner must be in line with the head noun of the NP and its feature of gender can guide the selection of the proper form of determiners. However, there are no changes in English determiners in form and gender.

The possessives are taken as an example to show the similarities and differences between the learners' native languages and the target language. The possessives can indicate definiteness in English. The possessives in Spanish and French can also perform the similar syntactic and semantic functions. They all indicate the ownership, but there are some differences at the same time.

Table 5.9 Possessive determiners in English, Spanish and French

<table>
<tr><th>Possessives in English</th><th>Possessives in Spanish</th><th>Possessives in French</th></tr>
<tr><td>my</td><td>mi or mis</td><td>mon, ma or mes</td></tr>
<tr><td>your (single)</td><td>tu or tus</td><td>ton, ta or tes</td></tr>
<tr><td>his</td><td rowspan="3">su or sus</td><td rowspan="3">son, sa or ses</td></tr>
<tr><td>her</td></tr>
<tr><td>its</td></tr>
<tr><td>our</td><td>nuestro, nuestra,
nuestros, or nuestras</td><td>notre or nos</td></tr>
<tr><td>your (plural)</td><td>vuestro, vuestra,
vuestros, or vuestras</td><td>votre or vos</td></tr>
<tr><td>their</td><td>suyo, suya, suyos,
or suyas</td><td>leur or leurs</td></tr>
</table>

As is shown in Table 5.9, the possessives in all these three languages express definiteness through modifying the owners of the nouns. However, the possessives in Spanish and French must match the gender and number of the nouns they describe, rather than the gender and number of the owners. According to Givon's (1990) criteria of markedness, possessives in Spanish and French tend to be more complex than their equivalents in English with respect to structural complexity. Moreover, Spanish and French possessives are less frequent in frequency distribution and cognitively more complex in terms of attention, mental effort or processing time than their corresponding structures in English. Therefore, the possessives in Spanish and French are more marked than English possessives. According to the third prediction of Eckman's MDH, "those areas of the target language which are different from the native language, but are not more marked than the native language, will not be difficult" (Eckman, 1977: 321). The accuracy of the item of other determiners of French and Spanish learners is 22.02%, higher than Chinese, but lower than native English speakers (35.11%). Moreover, there existed significant difference between the [+ART] group L2 learners and the native speakers in this item ($p=0.000$). This result seems to be unexpected. The low accuracy and the significant difference were mainly caused by the overuse of the definite article among Spanish and French L2 learners due to language transfer. It is illustrated in detail in the following part of overuse/underuse of articles.

5.4.2 Differences in Accuracy between Different Semantic Types

Table 5.7 shows the accuracy of different semantic types of

articles, which indicates that the accuracy of T4 was the highest and T3 was the lowest. Moreover, in the four types concerning SR and HK, it shows that all participants, regardless of native languages, had higher accuracy for the definite article and the zero article. The accuracy of the definite article in [+SR][+HK] were apparently higher than those in [−SR][+HK]. The accuracy of indefinite articles in [−SR][−HK] context was higher than the accuracy in [+SR][−HK] context and the accuracy of the other determiners was very low. However, the accuracy of the other determiners in [+SR][+HK] was higher than that in [+SR][−HK]. Differences in accuracy between different semantic types of articles and other determiners can also be explained through the analysis of language transfer and markedness.

Hsin (2007) made a comparison between Mandarin Chinese and English DPs. He classified English determiners and their correspondence in Chinese into four semantic types: referential definites, generics, referential indefinites and nonreferentials. As is shown in Table 5.10, the determiners of the participants' native languages and the target language were also classified into the above-mentioned four semantic types.

Table 5.10 Classification of semantic types of determiners①

Type	Chinese	English	Spanish	French
[−SR] [+HK]	1. bare N	1. a N [C] 2. the N [C] 3. bare N 4. the+*adj.*	1. el/la N[M]/[F] 2. los/las [M]/[F]	1. le/la N [M]/[F] 2. les Ns
[+SR] [+HK]	1. bare N 2. Det/Num +Cl+N	1. Det N	1. Det N [M]/[F]	1. Det N [M]/[F]
[+SR] [−HK]	1. Num+Cl +N	1. a N [C] 2. Ns [C] 3. bare N [U]	1. un/una N 2. unos/unas Ns	1. un/une N [M]/[F] 2. des Ns [Pl]
[−SR] [−HK]	1. Bare N	1. a N [C] 2. Ns [C] 3. bare N [U]	1. el/la N [M]/[F] 2. bare N 3. Ns/Nes	1. le N [M]/[F] 2. Ns [C] 3. du/de la N [M]/[F] 4. des Ns 5. bare N

N: noun　　Ns: plural noun
SR: specific reference　　HK: hearer's knowledge
Det: determiner　　Cl: classifier
Num: number

Although Chinese has no article system, a bare noun preceded by personal possessives, demonstratives or classifiers can indicate definiteness and specificity, just like the function of the definite article in English. English has one form to represent

① The classification of determiners and comparison between Chinese and English was extracted from Hsin (2007).

definiteness, whereas Chinese has two forms. Comparatively, the forms in Mandarin Chinese are less than those in English in [+SR][−HK] and [−SR][+HK]. Therefore, the presence of definiteness in Chinese implies the presence of definiteness in English, but the presence of definiteness in English does not imply the presence of definiteness in Chinese. According to Eckman's criteria of typological markedness, the definiteness in Chinese is more marked than in English. The higher accuracy in [+SR][+HK] can also be explained by Givon's criteria for Markedness: The DPs in Chinese with respect to structural complexity, frequency distribution and cognitive complexity are more marked than those in English in the context of [+SR][+HK]. Therefore, the DPs in [+SR][+HK] are more marked in Chinese than in English and the contrary is the case in the context of [−SR][+HK] and in [+SR][−HK]. As for the uses of generics, the opposite is the case. According to the third prediction of Eckman's MDH, "those areas of the target language which are different from the native language, but are not more marked than the native language, will not be difficult" (Eckman, 1977: P321). It explains why the accuracy of DPs of Chinese learners in [+SR][+HK] was apparently higher than that in [−SR][+HK] and in [+SR][−HK].

French L2 learners and the Spanish L2 learners had an overall better performance than Chinese learners on English article use. It can be explained by the fact that French and Spanish have an article system, which is the same as the target language. However, the accuracy of generics ([−SR][+HK]) was not high. It was caused by the overuse of the definite article in French and Spanish learners. There are four different forms to express generics in English, but generic reference can only be expressed by the definite article in Spanish and French and bare NPs are ungrammatical. According to the criteria of Eckman's typological markedness, French and Spanish are less marked than English in the usage of generics. According to Eckman's transferability in terms of markedness, French and Spanish learners tend to transfer the unmarked forms from their native language to the target language. Due to language transfer, French and Spanish learners tend to use the definite article instead of indefinite articles or the bare NPs. Moreover, in the type of [－SR][－HK], French and Spanish also use the definite article instead of the indefinite article. The frequency of the definite article in French and Spanish is higher than that in English, which explains why there existed overuse of definite article and underuse of indefinite article among the French and Spanish learners.

5.4.3 Overuse and Underuse of Articles among Learners with Different Native Languages

5.4.3.1 Overuse of the Definite Article

According to the results of the chi-square test in Table 5.8, all three groups of learners exhibited significant differences in terms of the definite article ($X^2=128.794$, $p=0.000$; $X^2=30.239$, $p=0.000$ and $X^2=30.893$, $p=0.000$ respectively) compared with the correct answers. Moreover, there was a tendency of overuse of the definite article in both [－SR][＋HK] and [＋SR][－HK], especially among Chinese learners.

Chinese learners failed to distinguish SR and HK in generic reference and it was difficult for them to identify countability when the reference was an uncountable noun. Chinese learners tend to think that a specific reference needs *the*. That leads to the overgeneralization of the definite article. Therefore, the overuse of *the* among Chinese learners is partly due to the failure to distinguish SR and HK of the NPs in English and partly due to the overgeneralization of the learned knowledge. Chinese learners tended to use bare NPs to signify definite and indefinite NPs. Overgeneralization and analogy might be learning strategies. Therefore, Chinese learners might overgeneralize the principles and overuse the definite article.

French and Spanish definite articles are usually used with a NP to refer to a specific reference when both the speaker and the hearer know what the referent is. Theoretically speaking, French and Spanish are more marked than English in terms of the usage of the definite article, since both languages have gender (masculine or feminine) and number (single or plural) in articles, while the English definite article *the* has no distinction of gender or number. According to the third prediction of Eckman's MDH, a structure in the target which is different from and not more marked than that in the native language will not be difficult for the L2 learners. Therefore, the unmarked usage of *the* should not be difficult to Spanish and French Speakers for what might lie in the differences between them. Unlike *the* in English, the French definite article is used with mass nouns, plural nouns or abstract nouns to express the generic reference. For instance:

2. (a) J'aime *le* lait. (I like milk.)

(b) J'aime *les* romans. (I like novels.)

(c) *Le* capitalisme a transformé ce pays. (Capitalism has transformed this country.)

In the above example, the generic reference in English is expressed by zero article, while in French the definite articles are used. That can explain why French learners overused the definite article *the* in the context of [−SR][+HK]. The possessive determiners in Spanish are used in most cases in the same way as they are used in English. However, it must be pointed out that in many instances—especially when referring to body parts, clothing or items that are closely associated with an individual—Spanish uses the definite articles (*el*, *la*, *los* or *las*), the equivalents of *the*, instead of possessive determiners. For example:

3. (a) *Tengo las manos frias*. (I have the hands cold.)

(b) *Tiene las manos frias*. (He has the hands cold.)

(c) *Tienen las manos frias*. (They have the hands cold.)

In the above examples, Spanish speakers are accustomed to using *las* (the) instead of *mis*, *sus* and *sus* (my, his and their) even where ambiguity is presented to English speakers. It leads to the overuse of the definite article for the Spanish L2 learners under the influence of their native language. Therefore, Spanish L2 learners unconsciously transferred the unmarked feature in their native language to the target language in the process of article acquisition. Furthermore, when the indefiniteness of the countable NPs or uncountable NPs is expressed, *some*, *any* or a zero article can be used in front of the NPs in English, the plural forms of the indefinite article *du*, *de la*, *de l'* or the partitive article *des* is used in French. There is no partitive article in English, therefore the French learners may refer to their native languages and overuse the indefinite article or the definite article when they can not find the equivalent.

Although overuse occurred among all the participants regardless of their native language, there was significant difference between [－ART] group (Chinese learners) and [+ART] group (Spanish, French learners and native English speakers) (p=0.000 and p=0.000 respectively). No difference was found within the [+ART] group L2 learners (p=0.892).

5.4.3.2 Underuse of the Indefinite Article and the Zero Article

As Table 5.8 shows, there existed underuse among both groups of Chinese learners and French and Spanish learners in the use of indefinite article. Furthermore, there existed significant differences (p = 0.000, 0.002) in the underuse between the two groups and the correct answer separately. The French and Spanish learners also have the tendency to underuse the zero article and the difference is significant (p = 0.004). However, there existed no significant difference between accuracy of Chinese learners and that of the correct answer in the use of the zero article.

The underuse of indefinite articles among Chinese L2 learners are caused by the countability of English nouns. Except the uncountable nouns, all the countable nouns need to be modified by a determiner. Except for the [+SR][+HK], the indefinite article can be used in the rest three semantic types in

English. For instance, the English indefinite article can be used in [−SR][+HK], while bare NPs in Chinese are used to refer to the generics. The English indefinite article can also be used in [+SR][−HK] and [−SR][−HK], while the corresponding expression in Chinese is the form of "Num + Cl. + N" or a bare N. Therefore, the frequency of bare NPs in Chinese is apparently higher than those in English and the frequency of *a/an* in English is higher than the frequency of bare Ns or the "Num+Cl+N" form in Chinese. Language transfer accounts for why there existed no significant difference between the accuracy of Chinese learners and the correct answer in the use of the zero article. There was underuse in indefinite article and the difference was significant.

The experimental results of underuse is partly consistent with the findings of some researchers (Master, 1997; Parrish, 1987) who reported that zero article dominated in all environments of L2 article acquisition among [−ART] group L2 learners, at least in the early stages. Parrish (1987) investigated the zero article from the perspective of acquisition order. He reported that the zero article was acquired first, followed by the definite article, and then the indefinite article. Similarly, Master (1997) claimed that, "the first article that seems to be acquired by [−ART] speakers is zero" (Master, 1997: 216). His data showed that overuse of zero decreased with an increase in proficiency level.

In English, the type of generics can be expressed in four different forms, including "the + N", "a/an + N", "bare N", "the + *adj.*". However, Spanish and French consistently and systematically use the definite article to mark a generic reference, which has already been mentioned in Chapter 4. French and Spanish are less marked than English in the usage of generics. Due to language transfer, French and Spanish learners tend to use definite article instead of indefinite articles or bare NPs. Furthermore, French and Spanish also make use of the definite article instead of the indefinite article in [−SR][−HK] context. For instance:

4. (a) quatre Euros le kilo (French)
   (b) cuatro Euros el kilo (Spanish)
   (c) four Euros a kilo (English)

The frequency of the definite article in French and Spanish is higher than that in English, which explains why there was overuse of the definite article but underuse of indefinite articles among French and Spanish learners.

5.5 Discussion

This chapter mainly focuses on the usage of articles and other determiners in the production of language learners' blank-filling task. The experiment explores the uses of articles as well as other determiners such as demonstratives and possessives which can exert similar functions before nouns to complement the analysis of articles. The relevant findings supplied positive evidence to answer the research questions raised at the beginning of this chapter.

The first question concerns the differences in accuracy of

articles between different semantic types. The experimental result shows that there existed difference in the accuracy of four semantic types. The accuracies of the definite article and the zero article in [+SR][+HK] were higher than their accuracies in [−SR][+HK] among all groups. Moreover, the accuracy of indefinite articles in [−SR][−HK] was higher than the accuracy in [+SR][−HK] context. The accuracies of the other determiners in [+SR][+HK] were also higher than in [+SR][−HK]. Although Chinese has no article system, a bare noun preceded by personal possessives, demonstratives or classifiers can play the similar functions of definiteness and specificity to the semantic functions of English determiners, including articles. Table 5.10 shows that the DPs in [+SR][+HK] in Chinese are more marked than in English and the contrary is the case in the context of [−SR][+HK] and in [+SR][−HK]. According to predictions of Eckman's MDH, if a structure in the target language is more marked than its corresponding structure in the learners' native language, it will be difficult for learners to acquire and the contrary is the case. That explains why the accuracies of DPs in [+SR][+HK] were apparently higher than in [−SR][+HK] and in [+SR][−HK].

The second question asks whether there exists overuse or underuse among the learners with different native languages. The overuse of the definite article in [−SR][+HK] was found in both the [+ART] group L2 learners, namely, French and Spanish learners and [−ART]group learners, namely, Chinese learners. It indicates that Chinese learners failed to distinguish SR and HK in the context of generics and it was difficult for them to identify countability when the reference was an uncountable noun. Chinese learners had a strong notion that a specific reference needed *the*. That leaded to the overgeneralization of *the*. Therefore, the overuse of *the* among Chinese learners was partly due to the failure to perceive SR and HK of the NPs in English and partly due to the overgeneralization of the learned knowledge. As for French and Spanish learners, the overuse of the definite article was caused by language transfer. The definite articles (including the masculine and feminine forms) are consistently used to refer to generics in French and Spanish. While in English, all forms of articles can be used to refer to generics. French and Spanish learners tended to transfer unmarked form in their native languages to the target language. The finding of overuse of the definite article in this experiment was confirmed by many studies. Many researchers (Brown, 1973; Warden, 1976; Huebner, 1983; Parrish, 1987, Master, 1987; Thomas, 1989; Liu and Gleason, 2002; Wang, 2005) have made studies to examine the overuse of the definite article which can generally be divided into two types:

(1) The overuse of *the* in [−SR][+HK]

Huebner (1983) made a longitudinal study of an adult Hmong English learner. He found that the learner used *the* in all language environments at the beginning period. And later this learner supplied *the* in the context of [−SR][+HK]. Master (1987) investigated the production of target English learners from five different native language backgrounds. Master also claimed that *the* is associated with the [−SR][+HK] context.

He claimed the overgeneralization of the definite article *the* in L2 learners. Huebner called this *the*-"flooding" and reported that the overgeneralization of the definite article is a dynamic process and *the*-"flooding" receded with the development of the learner's language proficiency. Huebner found that "the flood gradually receded, with the definite article disappearing first from [－SR][－HK] contexts, but persevering longer in [＋SR][－HK] contexts. His subject continued to use the definite article virtually exclusively in [＋SR][＋HK] and [－SR][＋HK] contexts at the end of the first year" (cited in Thomas, 1989: 340).

Liu and Gleason (2002) undertook a research that supported the ESL students' overuse of the definite article *the* in [－SR][＋HK]. The participants were asked to insert the definite article where they thought necessary and grouped the occurrences into four types, namely, cultural, structural, situational and textual use. It was found that the definite article *the* was overused in the context of [－SR][＋HK]. For instance, the participants inserted *the* in the following sentence: "At the zoo I saw several tigers. I think *the* tigers are beautiful animals". The researchers held the opinion that the definite article before the noun *tigers* was unnecessary overuse because the insertion of *the* turned the generic reference into specific reference, which changed the original meaning of the sentence.

Wang (2005) conducted another research that supported the findings of Liu and Gleason from a different aspect. He analyzed non-generic reference uses of the definite article in students' composition from Chinese learners' English Corpus (CLEC) with the same framework as that of Li and Gleason. The subjects were divided into three groups according to their different language proficiency. Through systematic statistical analyses he found that Chinese learners encountered different levels of difficulty in each group. He claimed that there was significant difference between English and Chinese in the uses of reference. The non-generic use of the definite article in English was more marked than Chinese which predicted the inevitable misuse in acquisition.

(2) The overuse of *the* in [+SR][−HK]

Many experimental studies revealed that the language learners tend to overuse the definite article in the context of [+SR][−HK](Brown, 1973; Warden, 1976; Huebner, 1983; Parrish, 1987, Thomas, 1989). Parrish (1987) made a longitudinal study of English by a Japanese English learner and analyzed reasons for the overuse of the definite article. Parrish found 9.4% of the overuse occurred in the contexts of [+SR][−HK]. He claimed that the abundant use of *the* in [+SR][−HK] was not totally random even though the article choice of this learner was not target-like. It was systematic and governed by the semantic functions of NPs and it was the "evidence of the learner's attempt to maintain internal consistency" (Parrish, 1987: 361).

Thomas (1989) also made a study to investigate the acquisition of the English article system. Making use of Huebner's semantic classification, Thomas classified the noun phrases into four semantic types. The 30 adult subjects in his study were divided into two groups: [+ART] group and

[−ART] group. The former group includes 1 French, 1 German, 1 Greek, 2 Italians and 2 Spanish and the latter group contains 13 Japanese, 6 Chinese, 3 Koreans and 1 Finnish. The subjects were subclassified into three groups according to the language proficiency of the language learners. The result showed that the language learners whose native language had the article system presented similar pattern of development in terms of the usage of *a* and *the*. The [+ART] group made use of *the* and *a* more frequently than the [− ART] group in appropriate contexts. Thomas explained that learners associated *the* with [+SR], but not [+HK] and they could appropriately use *a* in the [− HK] context. His research is not consistent with Master's conclusion that *the* is associated with [+HK] rather than [+SR]. At the same time his research did not find the flooding of *the* as claimed by Huebner in the [+SR][−HK] context. He explained that "it may be that L2 learners, like L1 learners, associate *the* with the feature of [+SR], and later learn the relevance of the feature [±HK] to the English article system" (Thomas, 1989: 352). Thomas pointed out that child learners of native language frequently used the definite article in the contexts of referential indefinites ([+SR][−HK]) where adults usually use the indefinite article. He also found that adult L2 learners were inclined to overgeneralize the definite article. His research showed that the rates of the definite article in referential indefinite context produced by his 30 L2 learners with different native languages were significantly higher than in nonreferential context ([− SR][− HK]). Different from Huebner's and Master's finding that *the* was related with the contexts of generics ([−SR][+HK]), Thomas (1989) reported the overuse of *the* in referential indefinite ([+SR][−HK]) contexts.

Ionin (2006) conducted a research to explore the evidence for the reality of specificity. His participants were adult English learners whose native languages were Russian and Korean which lack articles. The results showed that "the learners' errors are tied to specificity of the reference: they consist largely of overuse of *the* in specific indefinite context and overuse of *a* in non-specific definite context" (Ionin, 2006:175).

The above mentioned studies investigate transferability from the perspective of the binary feature of [±SR] and [±HK], and the present study explores the transferability from the perspective of markedness. The overuse of *the* in [−SR][+HK] in this experiment is consistent with the findings of Huebner (1983) and Master (1988), but different from Thomas' (1989) findings.

The third question relates to how language transfer happens due to different degree of markedness in article acquisition. In the previous chapter, it was found that the transferability of the native language depends on the markedness degree between the target language and the learners' native language. In that case, how the occurrence of language transfer correlates with markedness is the concern of this question. The cross-linguistic comparison between the learners' native languages and the target language in Table 5.10 shows the relationship between transferability and markedness. French and Spanish learners tended to use the definite article instead of indefinite articles or bare nouns, while Chinese learners were prone to use bare nouns to refer to generics. It indicates that whether language transfer will occur and when it happens depend on the cross-linguistic comparison of the markedness and the degree of markedness between the target language and the learners' native language. Furthermore, language learners tended to transfer unmarked forms rather than marked forms from their native language to the target language. Then what metalinguistic knowledge is involved in the participants' article selection? Is the correlation between language transfer and markedness systematic in language learners' intuition? These questions are to be answered by interviewing the participants in the previous two experiments in the next chapter.

Chapter 6 The Interviews

The previous two experiments are mainly quantitative analyses of the use of articles by L1 and L2 English learners. However, the production data may not present a true picture of the learners' acquisition, because they may have avoided the uses they are not sure of. Therefore, interviews which are more qualitative in nature are necessary to support the quantitative research. Semi-structured interviews were conducted in this chapter to investigate the reasons for the participants' choices and to get information about the metalinguistic knowledge involved in the participants' decision-making. Specific, non-specific reasons as well as reasons related to language transfer and markedness were analyzed.

6.1 Research Questions

The interviews aim to investigate the intuition of learners in the process of article selection. It also aims to find whether language transfer and markedness are selectively and systematically correlated in article selection. Three questions are addressed in this chapter:

(1) What metalinguistic knowledge is involved in the participants' article selection?

(2) Are there any differences between language learners with different native languages in their way of choosing the articles?

(3) Is the correlation between language transfer and markedness systematic in language learners' intuition?

6.2 Research Method

6.2.1 Participants and Procedure

After the completion of the previous two experiments, four participants (1 Native speaker, 1 French, 1 Spanish and 1 Chinese respectively) were invited to attend a semi-structured interview to state the reasons for their choices in the previous two experiments. If the participants could not state specific reasons, they were instructed to tell the researcher that they had simply guessed it or there was no clue. The interview was conducted in English and each interview lasted about an hour. The learners were sometimes interrupted by the researcher for the clarification of ambiguous statements and were asked some related questions. With the consent of the participants, the interviews were recorded and transcribed. The transcription notation was cited from Allwright and Bailey (1991) (see Appendix C).

6.2.2 Classification of the Reasons

The intrinsic reasons for the learners' choices are explored in this chapter. The reasons are broadly classified into two types: specific reasons and non-specific reasons. The specific reasons are divided into four subtypes: referential definites, generics, referential indefinites and nonreferential. The non-specific reasons were divided into three subtypes: plausible choice, elimination, and no clue.

The broad classification of the reasons and that of the non-specific reasons in this study were borrowed from Butler's (2002) coding for the metalinguistic analysis of English article use. Butler (2002) classified reasons for article use provided by the learners into specific and non-specific reasons. Since he believed that the metacognitive knowledge of language learners lied in the misuse of articles, he classified the reasons for article choice based on the misuse of articles. The former type included problems with referentiality, misdetection of countability, nongeneralizable or idiosyncratic hypotheses, and other reasons. The latter type consisted of reasons based on any of the following three factors: plausible choice, elimination, and no clue. For the purpose of this study, the specific reasons for article choices are further divided into four groups based on their semantic features, which is different from Buttler's classification. Furthermore, the present study adds a particular factor that includes both the specific and the non-specific reasons: language transfer, as can be seen from Table 6.1.

Table 6.1 Classification of the reasons①

Reason category		Description	Examples
Specific reasons	[+SR][+HK]	The learners were able to identify rules of grammar or other reasons for selecting the articles they chose.	I choose *the* because it's a particular book mentioned before.
	[−SR][+HK]		It refers to all the bikes, the whole kind of bikes.
	[+SR][−HK]		It is mentioned for the first time.
	[−SR][−HK]		I choose *a*, because it means per hour.
Non-specific reasons	plausible choice	The learners could not identify any specific reasons for their article choices.	It sounds like it should be this article.
	elimination		Others don't work, so I think that this article is the only choice, although I don't know why this is right.
	no clue		I have no idea, so I just picked one.

① The examples of non-specific reasons are extracted from Butler (2002).

Language transfer	Specific reasons	The learners made the choice by comparing their native languages and the target language.	I definitely choose this, because it has got the same expression in Spanish/French/Chinese.
	Non-specific reasons		I'm not sure. I refer to Spanish/French/Chinese.

With the classification of the reasons for learners to make their choices, we can have a clear view of the distribution of reasons and the rates of accuracy to have a better understanding of the learners' metalinguistic knowledge in article selection.

6.3 Results

6.3.1 Descriptive Analysis of Specific and Non-specific Reasons

The distribution of specific and non-specific reasons in different groups is summarized in Table 6.2. The descriptive statistics provides an overall description of the metalinguistic understanding of each participant. It must be pointed out that the frequency of reasons refers to the number of the participants' choices, rather than the accurate numbers.

Table 6.2 Frequency of specific and non-specific reasons

Explanation		Groups			
		Chinese	Spanish	French	Native speaker
Non-specific	Frequency	44	32	37	45
	Percentage	42.3%	30.8%	35.6%	43.3%
Specific	Frequency	60	72	67	59
	Percentage	57.7%	69.2%	64.4%	56.7%

As is shown in Table 6.2, all the participants with different native languages gave more specific reasons (57.7%, 69.2%, 64.4%, and 56.7% respectively) than non-specific ones for their choices. The participants went for plausible choices, elimination, or had no clue in fewer instances (42.3%, 30.8%, 35.6%, and 43.3%). It shows that the percentage of specific reasons of all the participants outnumbered the non-specific reasons. As for the learners with different native languages, the Spanish learner and the French learner stated more specific reasons than the Chinese learner and the native speaker, accounting for 69.2% and 64.4% respectively. The percentage of non-specific reasons for the native speaker was higher than L2 English learners.

Frequency of the reasons for the learners to make their choices does not equate to the accuracy of their choices. Whether the reasons stated by the participants helped them to make accurate choices is shown in the following table.

Table 6.3 Accuracy of the answers in specific and non-specific reasons

Explanation		Groups			
		Chinese	Spanish	French	Native speaker
Non-specific	Frequency of reasons	18	23	28	41
	Accuracy of answers	40.9%	71.8%	75.7%	91.1%
Specific	Frequency of reasons	43	55	50	55
	Accuracy of answers	71.7%	76.4%	74.6%	93.2%

Table 6.3 shows that the native speaker produced the highest accuracy in both specific and non-specific reasons (93.2% and 91.1% respectively). Articles chosen by the Spanish learner and the French learner with non-specific reasons were mostly accurate. Furthermore, the Spanish and French learners showed high similarity both in specific and non-specific reasons. The Chinese participant produced the lowest accuracy (40.9% and 71.7% respectively). To further investigate why the participants made their choices, the researcher divided the specific reasons into four types and the non-specific reasons into three. Figures 6.1 and 6.2 indicate the frequency and accuracy of subtypes of specific reasons and non-specific reasons.

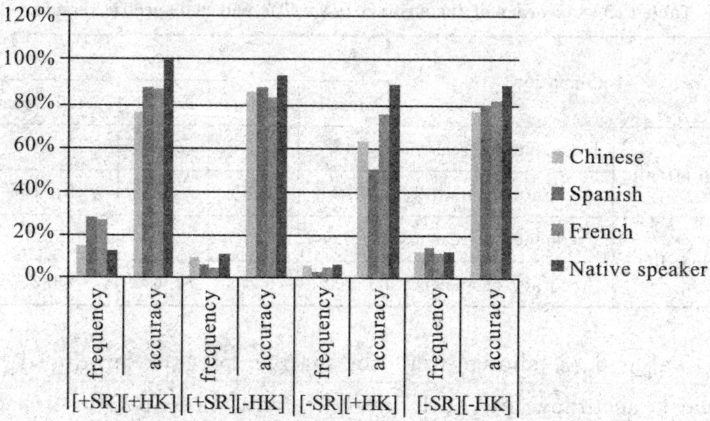

Figure 6.1 Frequency and accuracy of subtypes of specific reasons

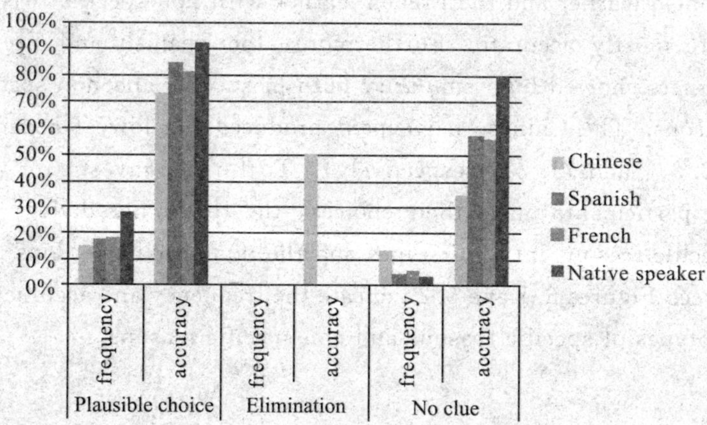

Figure 6.2 Frequency and accuracy of subtypes of non-specific reasons

In terms of specific reasons, the percentage of the subtype [+SR][+HK] was the highest (14.6%, 27.8%, 26.4%, and 12.5% respectively). In other words, the participants could verbalize their reasons behind their choices in the context of referential definites. The accuracy order of the four types of specific reasons is referential definites ([+SR][+HK]), nonreferential([−SR][−HK]), referential indefinites ([+SR][−HK]), and generics ([−SR][+HK]). Of all the subtypes, the frequency of the generics ([−SR][+HK]) was the lowest except for the French learner. The accuracy of these four subtypes generally followed the same order except the Chinese learner. The highest accuracy of the Chinese learner is referential indefinites ([+SR][−HK]) instead of referential definites ([+SR][+HK]). The table shows that most of the articles chosen with specific reasons were accurate.

Among non-specific reasons, the frequencies of plausible choices were the highest (15.3%, 17.4%, 18.1% and 27.8% respectively) for all the participants. Compared with L2 English learners, the native speaker showed stronger tendency in employing the plausible choice in non-specific reasons. Of the three types of non-specific reasons, the factor of elimination had the lowest ratios. None of the participants except the Chinese L2 English learner (1.4%) used the method of elimination to make the choices. The Chinese learner cited "no clue" more frequently than other groups of learners. The accuracies of plausible choices of all participants were higher than the factors of elimination and no clue and that of the native speaker was extremely high (92.5%). These results suggest that the participants whose native languages have an article system utilized more implicit knowledge than explicit knowledge. Although they could not verbalize the reasons for article selections, they could make the correct choices based on their implicit knowledge. The Chinese learner failed to articulate metalinguistic explanation and the accuracy for non-specific reasons they provided was relatively low.

The above distribution of frequency and accuracy of specific and non-specific reasons is different from the findings reported in Butler (2002) and Lee (2013). Butler (2002) interviewed Japanese learners of English after the participants completed a fill-in-the-blank task and asked for reasons behind their article choices. He reported that the learners at higher proficiency levels tended to offer more specific reasons for their selection of articles (65%) than the learners at lower proficiency levels (44%). Lee (2013) investigated metalinguistic knowledge of Korean learners at various proficiency levels in acquiring English articles. It was found in his experiment that specific reasons accounted for 78.4% of the article choices while 21.6% were made with non-specific reasons. Among the participants in the present interviews, the native speaker possessed the highest language proficiency, the French and the Spanish came to the second, and the Chinese learner's language proficiency was the lowest. Different from Butler's and Lee's findings, it was found in the present interviews that the native speaker cited more non-specific reasons and the French and the Spanish gave more specific reasons. It is possibly caused by different native languages of the participants. The participants of Butler's and Lee's experiments were all L2 learners, while the participants in this study include the native speakers. It was found that the native speaker used more implicit knowledge in the process of his article selection. As for the L2 learners, it is similar to the findings of Butler and

Lee, because the French and the Spanish learners who had higher language proficiency stated more specific reasons than the Chinese learner.

6.3.2 Descriptive Analysis of Language Transfer

As for the reason of language transfer, the percentage for the Chinese interviewee to refer to her native language takes 11.5%. The percentage of the Spanish interviewee is 26% and for French, 22.1%. It shows that language transfer happened more frequently in the French and the Spanish learner than the Chinese learner. There also existed difference in terms of the accuracy. The accuracies of the French and the Spanish learner were 82.6% and 77.8% respectively, much higher than that of the Chinese learner (58.3%).

Table 6.4 Frequency and accuracy of language transfer

Explanation		Groups			
		Chinese	Spanish	French	Native speaker
Language transfer	Frequency	12	27	23	
	Percentage	11.5%	26%	22.1%	
Language transfer	Accuracy	7	21	19	
	Percentage	58.3%	77.8%	82.6%	

Through the above descriptive analyses, three conclusions can be made. First, as Table 6.2 shows, the participants gave more specific reasons for their choices of articles than non-specific reasons. Second, the frequency for the participants to make the plausible choices in non-specific reasons was the highest and the frequency of the subtype of [+SR][+HK] was the highest in specific reasons. Third, the percentages of reasons attributed to language transfer of French and Spanish learners whose native languages have an article system were higher than that of the Chinese learner.

6.4 Data Analysis

The aim of the qualitative analysis of the interview is mainly to further reveal the learners' metalinguistic knowledge with regard to their article selection. It aims to explore whether there exist some systematic differences between the learners with different native languages. The responses from the participants to the question "what is the reason for you to give your answer" offered some valuable information to analyze the metalinguistic knowledge of the learners . The following are some records of the interviews. The letter "R" symbolizes the researcher and the different letters are the abbreviations of different native languages of the participants (N stands for native English speakers, F for French, S for Spanish and C for Chinese).

6.4.1 Different Types of Reasons: Specific Reasons

The language learners with different native languages showed the same confidence and could, in most cases, offer specific reasons to explain why they made the choice of the definite article in the type of [+SR][+HK] and indefinite articles in [+SR][-HK] and [-SR][-HK].

The participants generally gave specific reasons to choose the definite article in [+SR][+HK], especially in T1S1 (specific referents assumed known to the hearer) and T1S2 (referent previously mentioned in the discourse). At the same time, the accuracy in [+SR][+HK] was the highest in four subtypes of specific reasons. For example, all the participants provided specific reasons for the first sentence (*Let's go to ________ cinema—that'll take your mind off the problem for a while.*).

N: *Number One, the sentence shows them first that they, em... referring to = a = specific cinema that both people already are aware of this prior knowledge so... eh...*

C: *No. 1 I choose the, because this is the specific cinema that both the speaker and the listener know in the context, so...*

S: *The first one, [er] I choose C, because = when they = want to say let's go to the cinema that'll take your mind. So I said "the" because I want to refer to the very cinema.*

F: *Let's go to the cinema. "the" because in French, [laugh] in articles, it is a usual usage.*

All the participants stated specific reasons and all made the accurate choice to select *the* in [+SR][+HK]. Moreover, both the native speaker and the Chinese learner paid attention to the factors of SR and HK and expressed the confidence of their choices. The confidence of the participants is in line with the accuracy of the definite article in [+SR][+HK] (Chinese 76.20%, Spanish 87.50%, French 86.80% and the Native speaker 100%). Furthermore, the result is also in accord with the results of the second experiment in Chapter 5: all the learnersdemonstrated high accuracy in using the definite article in the context of [+SR][+HK] (Chinese 61.8%, French and Spanish 64.6%, and native speakers 93.8% respectively).

However, the native speaker and the L2 learners offered different explanations as for the zero article to refer to the definite referential. For instance, The participants cited different reasons for their selections in No. 16 (*By nine o'clock, all the Olympic torch bearers had reached the top of ________ Mount Qomolangma on which appeared a rare rainbow soon.*) and No. 17 (________ *Boxing Day, when Christmas boxes used to be given to servants, is the day following ________ Christmas Day.*). The native speaker provided the specific reason to make the choice while the L2 learners stated non-specific reasons.

N: (By nine o'clock, all the Olympic torch bearers had reached the top of Mount Qomolangma) Yeah, because It's a specific, eh, if it was, em, =if=that wasn't its name it would have been "the top of the mountain" and then probably as a clause it has been... like... the highest mountain in the world. It's a specific name so it goes the zero article rather than being an item of something that... then again Boxing Day is a name so it's zero article. (Uh-huh) and then you go the clause afterwards so it seems that one would be on their way round. Boxing Day, when Christmas boxes used to be given to servants, is a day following Christmas Day. They are both specific days, so they both have zero articles.

R: So you usually say Christmas Day and Boxing Day=but=you do not mean...

N: Yeah, we wouldn't say "the Boxing Day" or "a Boxing

Day" because "a Boxing Day" will refer to that there are several throughout the year but there is only one. The same is Christmas Day.

R: What about the definite article "the"?

N: You wouldn't say "the Boxing Day" because you wouldn't say "the Christmas Day" = It's = like that one, you wouldn't say "the Mount" = you = might say "the mountain" but then you have to make it a clause to refer to its name.

R: Now what about Christmas Day?

N: Eh, again the same It's zero article It's a specific day and it has a name = It's = sort of something like being called Abraham Lincoln you wouldn't say "the Abraham Lincoln" because that's referring to the president.

The native English speaker stated specific reasons for his choice. He knew that *Mount Qomolangma*, *Christmas Day* and *Boxing Day* were all specific references known both by the speaker and the hearer at the same time, therefore, he definitely made the choice of zero article in the context of [+SR][+HK]. As for the interviewer's question why he had not chosen *the* to refer to the definite referential, he did not offer a reasonable explanation. It indicates that the native speaker employed more implicit knowledge in the process of selection and could not verbalize reasons for his choice. Different from the native speaker, the L2 learners provided non-specific reasons. There existed language transfer in the French and Spanish participants and the Chinese learner showed heavy dependence on the grammar they were taught in class.

The participants generally gave specific reasons in [+SR]

[－HK] in which a specific referent yet unknown to the hearer was mentioned for the first time or the weak version of *one* was implied. For example, in No. 31 (*I ate* ________ *sandwich while I was waiting for the 20:08 train.*), all the participants were aware of the fact that the referent was mentioned for the first time and implied the weak version of *one*:

R: Are you sure your answer is right?

C: Yes, I am sure. Is it the right answer? [*laugh*] *a sandwich maybe refers to one sandwich.*

S: I ate a sandwich, one sandwich; It's not the sandwich [*laugh*], *one sandwich, now I choose A.*

F: I ate a sandwich while I was waiting for the 20:08 train. "The" means the specific one. I choose "a", but I can't explain why.

N: I ate a sandwich while I was waiting for the 20:08 train. Yeah, eh. Again that one could be "the sandwich" if you are referring to the sandwich that you both are aware of like is a package of sandwich that she is asking oh yeah, the sandwich while I was waiting for the train. Eh, but that because would be referring to an activity he is doing while waiting for the train. So I ate a sandwich while I was waiting for the train. So it could be either but then you need to know more information around that sentence, the context of that sentence for to be automatically... So there is none context you could go with either "a" or "the" depending on whether the other person is aware of the sandwich which is mentioned beforehand. Yeah.

In the above example, all the L2 learners chose *a*, because they assumed that the nominal *sandwich* was mentioned for the first time and the indefinite article *a* implied the meaning of *one*. The indefinite article *a* used as a weak version of *one* is one of the basic rules of articles introduced in ESL textbooks. Therefore, it seems that L2 learners were aware of this rule and applied it appropriately. It can explain the high accuracy of the indefinite article *a* in [+SR][−HK] in the first experiment in Chapter 4. Different from the L2 learners, the native speaker was aware of the SR and HK distinction. He hesitated as to whether *a* or *the* was the correct answer because he put the sentence in discourse and was considering whether the word *sandwich* had been mentioned before and whether the hearer was aware of that. His answer was *a* in the first experiment and he explained that he assumed that it was mentioned for the first time. One interesting thing is that although the participants all provided specific reasons in [+SR][−HK] when the indefinite article should be used, the accuracy of *an* in [+SR][−HK] in the second experiment was not high. As a matter of fact, its error rate was among the highest. It is mainly caused by the influence of language transfer, which will be explained in detail in the following section.

Furthermore, the participants all gave specific reasons for their choices of the indefinite article in the context of [−SR][−HK]. For example, in the sentence No. 43 (*The rice cost one dollar ________ pound.*), all the participants stated the specific reason:

R: Okay. And No. 43?

N: I'd (x) with "per pound" because it's "per" amount but equally as much you can use "a", "one dollar a pound".

C: *No. 43*, *em*, *⟨5⟩ pound refers to the weight*, *one dollar one pound*, *so I definitely choose A*, *a pound*.

S: *For each dollar cost me one pound*, *ok*, *a pound*, *I choose. "a" means each or one*.

F: *The rice cost one dollar ________ pound. I choose the answer. "one dollar a pound" means every or per*.

The explanations of the participants are coincidentally similar to each other, that is, *a* refers to *per* or *every*. They all gave specific reasons for their choices. It indicates that the learners all acquired the use of the indefinite article in the context of [−SR][−HK]. This explanation also confirms the result in the first experiment, and explains why the percentage of the accuracy of the subtype T4S1 was the highest. The confidence expressed by all participants in [−SR][−HK] was due to language transfer which will be explained in the part of language transfer and markedness.

6.4.2 Different Types of Reasons: Non-specific Reasons

As for the non-specific reasons, different participants gave different reasons for their choices. It demonstrated that the participants tended to turn to their implicit knowledge when they were not sure about the answers.

The Chinese learner was strongly influenced by the grammatical rules that she had learned from her English teachers or textbooks. In other words, she depended heavily on the grammatical rules that she had learned. When she was not sure about the answer, she turned to her intuition. For instance:

C: =*No. 33*. =*I think it is a specific reference*, *but there is no clue.* 〈5〉 *in fact I hesitated here to choose A or C, because =I=, according to my sense of language, it should be A, If it refers to the particular watch the man took out, it should be C. [laugh] I have learned English for so many years, (and) I don't know wether the accuracy of my sense of language can be better than the grammatical rules I learned. So I choose A.*

In the above example, the Chinese learner showed a conflicting mental experience when there existed contradiction between the grammar rules that she had learned from class instruction and the intuition that she had acquired during the process of acquiring the article system. Her explanation for another item also exhibits the same pattern:

C: No. 40, there is no articles in front of musical instrument.

C: No. 42, play the violin is a collocation, But 〈5〉 *if it is the case, I turn back to No. 40, play the violin is =a collocation =, but is it necessary to add an article before the musical instruments?*

R: to add or not to add? Are you sure about No. 42?

C: Play piano, play the piano 〈5〉, *It needs to add "the" according to my sense of language.*

R: You are not sure about the grammar that you learned?

C: I forgot it. I remember "the" =seems to= be added in front of musical instruments. I'm not sure.

In items No. 40 and No. 42, the answers offered by the Chinese learner seem to be contradictory. In No. 40, she chose the zero article before the musical instruments according to the vague memory of grammatical rules. However, in No. 42, she thought the definite article *the* should be used before the word *violin* which was also a musical instrument. It proves that the judgement she made based on her sense of language is more accurate than that based on the grammatical rules which is more difficult to be memorized. Therefore, for the Chinese learner, there is a noticeable feature: she was prone to depend heavily on the syntactic rules rather than the dynamic context. When she tried to decide whether a reference was specific or not, she usually referred to the clues attached to the reference she had learned in class.

The French participant also stated non-specific reasons when he was not sure about the reason for his choice. When he could not remember the grammar he had learned in classroom instruction, he turned to the implicit knowledge in his interlanguage. For instance:

F: *By nine o'clock, all the Olympic torch bearers had reached the top of Mount Qomolangma on which appeared a rare rainbow soon. I don't know.*

R: *You're not quite sure about this one?*

F: *No, I am not sure.*

R: *In French, how do you express it?*

F: *The Mount Qomolangma.*

R: *You choose "the" in French. Why did you choose zero in English?*

F: *... I don't know. Just sounds good without "the". Sometimes, It's a feeling.*

In this example, the French learner could not remember whether *the* should be used before the proper noun *Mount*

Qomolangma, therefore he turned to intuition, which draws largely on the implicit knowledge in article selection. The Spanish learner offered a different explanation. When he was not sure about the answer, he turned to his native language and negative transfer happened:

S: The Mount, yeah, the mount, I want to (×××) to say C, here,... is the mount, sorry, one mount. Only one Mount. The Mount Qomolangma, It's differ (ent) It's difficult to pronounce, [laugh] Qomolangma. (×××) The Boxing Day and the Christmas Day.. So I choose A, the, the.

R: Well, em, how do you just say that Day is Spanish? (×××) Is there also an article?

S: Yes,

R: Before Christmas Day?

S: Yeah (×××). (×××) with Christmas. Em, we say the Christmas Day (×××). Here is the same. For me, it sounds good. But I don't know why [laugh]. It's only for me. It sounds (×××) Ok.

Apparently the Spanish learner gave a plausible reason for his choice. He chose the definite article *the* to express the specific reference but not the zero article. He was aware of definiteness rather than the factor of hearer's knowledge. At the same time, he resorted to his native language when he forgot the rules in the textbook and the negative language transfer occured unconsciously.

6.4.3 Different Types of Reasons: Language Transfer and Markedness

Apart from specific and non-specific reasons, the particular reasons of language transfer for the participants' selection were also counted. The percentage for the Chinese learner to refer to her native language accounted for 11.5%. 26% of the reasons were given by the French learner who turned to his native language when making a choice and 22.1% for the Spanish. It shows that language transfer happened in the process of L2 learners' article selection. The interview of the participants also indicates that language transfer affected the choice of the learners with different native languages. For instance, both the French and the Spanish learner referred to their native languages and language transfer happened when they selected the answer for the sentence No. 35 (*There is* ________ *"h" in the word "honest".*)

F: *There is a "h" in the word "honest". Because it is "h".*

R: *Do you know when should we use a or an?*

F: *Yes. It depends on the next word, pronunciation and grammar.*

R: *When should we use a or an?*

F: *I can't remember.*

R: *When did you learn that? In primary school or in middle school?*

F: *In primary school...*

In the item No. 35, the French learner made a wrong choice, choosing *a* instead of *an* in front of the letter "h". And even in his explanation, he also said "*there is a 'h' in the word 'honest'*". In French, the indefinite article has two forms: *un* and *une*, which can identify the gender of the NPs. In English, the indefinite article also has two forms: *a* and *an*. Different from French, the choice of the two different forms in English depends on the pronunciation of the following word. Therefore, the selection of *a* or *an* in English and the selection of *un* or *une* in French have different rules. The usage of *an* in the target language (English) is more marked than the native language of the French learner. This result can be explained by the second prediction of Eckman's in his MDH: the relative degree of learning difficulty will correspond to the relative degree of the markedness. The relative degree of difficulty of the use of *an* in English is more marked than *un* and *une* in French, which predicts more difficulty for the French learner to acquire it. The French learner showed psychological difficulty in acquiring the usage of indefinite article *an* in the [+SR][−HK], which is in accordance with the high error rate of *an* in Experiment 1. The Spanish learner made the right choice, but the same mistake appeared when he explained thc reason for his choice:

S: *And the training is running fifty miles.. an hour. I thought=it=would be per hour, yeah, per hour. Per hour or an hour is the same.*

R: *Do you know when should we use a or an in English?*

S: *Yes, It is determined by the pronunciation of the next word. There is a "h" in the word hour. It is silent, so the word starts with a vowel, so I choose an.*

The Spanish learner knew the right answer should be *an*,

but when he explained the reason, he also said a "h" like the French learner. Both of them knew the rule for the use of *an*, but the rule was learned from class instruction or text books. *An hour* is NP which occurs frequently, therefore the Spanish learner kept firmly in mind that the right answer should be *an*. However, when he came across a word that was not in common usage, negative transfer of his native language happened and he made a mistake.

The same phenomenon of language transfer appeared for the use of the definite article in sentence No. 40 (*His mother taught ________ piano, but his father was only a blue-collar worker.*):

S: *I have doubt here [laugh], because (×××) like Spanish, we say the piano.*

R: *In Spanish, you really say the piano?*

S: *Yeah.*

R: *What about in English?*

S: *Em, (×××) [laugh]... Yeah, I think I'm quite sure in that.*

R: *=I= just wonder whether when you are saying play football whether there is an article between play and football in Spanish?*

S: *No, =no article=, so is the same as English, (×××) football, play football. Some of his friends said he could not play.. [em] the piano, the violin. So, C, my answer is C.*

In this item, the Spanish learner made the right choice for the reason that his native language Spanish also has the same expression. Like English, Spanish is also a language with a definiteness-based article system. In Spanish, we find the equivalent of the English NP "*the piano*". Furthermore, the definite article has two different forms in Spanish: *el* and *la* to distinguish genders. According to Givon's criteria of Markedness Theory, the definite article in Spanish is more complex in structure than that in English, and it tends to be cognitively more complex in terms of attention, mental effort or processing time. Therefore, the definite article in Spanish with respect to structural complexity, frequency distribution and cognitive complexity is more marked than that in English. According to the third prediction of Eckman's MDH, "those areas of the target language which are different from the native language, but are not more marked than the native language, will not be difficult" (Eckman, 1977: 321). This explains why the Spanish participant made the right choice: positive language transfer of his native language influenced his selection due to different markedness between the native language and the target language.

Chinese does not have an article system; however, there exist other determiners which can play similar referential functions in sentences. When the Chinese learner could find an equivalent in her native language to express the similar meaning, she tended to state specific reasons. For example, *the* in [+SR] [+HK] is similar to "*zhe*"(this) or "*na*" (that) in Chinese and *a* in [+SR][−HK] is similar to the meaning of a weak version of "*yi*" (one) in Chinese. Therefore, when she could find the equivalents in her native language, it was easier for her to remember the rules and she showed confidence to make the choice. On the contrary, when she could not find the equivalents in her native language, she had to refer to the rote memory of the grammatical rules that she had learned. For instance, in No. 43, the Chinese participant stated the specific reason:

C: *No. 43, em, ⟨5⟩ pound refers to the weight, one dollar one pound, so I definitely choose A, a pound.*

In this item, the Chinese participant could find the equivalent for the indefinite article *a*, the numeral in Chinese *yi*, therefore, she could "definitely" make the choice. However, when her native language had no equivalent, she became confused, hesitating whether the definite article should be used:

C: Play piano, play the piano ⟨5⟩, It needs to add "the" according to my sense of language.

R: You are not sure about the grammar that you learned?

C: I forgot it. I remember "the" = seems to = be added in front of musical instruments. I'm not sure.

In this part, when the Chinese participant could not find the equivalent in her native language she had to refer to the rules she had learned in class instruction. However, it was difficult for her to remember the rules of whether the definite article *the* should be put before the musical instruments after having learned them for so many years.

The finding that language transfer affects language learners' selection of articles was in accordance with the findings of Ionin et al. (2007). Ionin et al. (2007) conducted an experimental study to find the factors influencing article acquisition. Their study examined patterns of misuse of English articles among Spanish learners and Russian learners. It was found that Spanish learners transferred the semantic features of Spanish articles to

English, while Russian learners demonstrated fluctuation between the features of definiteness and specificity. They attributed the acquisition of articles to the interaction of three linguistic sources: UG, L1 transfer and L2 input. They claimed that L1 transfer plays an essential role in the process of article acquisition. It was also found in this study that the French and the Spanish English learner transferred the semantics in their native language to the acquisition of the target language. Similar to Ionin's finding, language transfer was also found in the Chinese participant, although it was not as obvious as the French and the Spanish learners whose native languages contained an article system. It showed that the Chinese learner was sure about her choices and stated specific reasons when she could find other determiners in Chinese to play similar functions as articles in English.

6.5 Discussion

This study examined the metalinguistic knowledge and the understanding of the English article system language learners used in the process of finishing the passage. It aims to find when and how language transfer and markedness function in this process.

Three research questions were raised in this chapter. The first question concerns metalinguistic knowledge involved in article acquisition. It was found that native English speakers could detect SR and HK successfully. It was also found that language transfer played a part in the process of L2 learners' selection of articles. The learners' selections were influenced by similarities or differences between the native language and the target language. For instance, the participants showed much confidence in choosing *the* in [+SR][+HK] and the indefinite article in [+SR][−HK] and [−SR][−HK]. There are corresponding demonstratives in Chinese and articles in French and Spanish which function similarly in NPs and it is easy for language learners to detect the definiteness and specificity in the target language. It accounts for the high accuracy of *the* in [+SR][+HK] and explains why all the participants showed confidence when they chose *the* in [+SR][+HK]. Similarly, there are corresponding numerals in these languages which exert the same function as the indefinite article in English. That is why the participants were also confident when they chose *a/an* in [+SR][−HK] and [−SR][−HK]. However, the confidence in their selection did not guarantee accuracy. The accuracy of their choices was determined by degree of markedness between the target language and the learners' native language.

The second question asks whether there exist differences between language learners with different native languages in their ways of choosing the articles. It demonstrated that differences occurred in the participants' article selection: the native speaker was less restricted by grammatical rules; the French English learner and the Spanish English learner tended to compare the article structures in English with those in their native languages; the Chinese English learner was strongly influenced by the grammatical rules learned in class and exhibited difficulty detecting the SR, HK and countability.

The native speaker realized that he could not depend exclusively on the structural rules or local context in choosing articles. He was unaware of English syntactic rules of articles sometimes and made article choices correctly but unconsciously. The native speaker gave more unspecific reasons in the selection of articles. Unlike L2 learners, he acquired the English article system at an early age. It was the competence of the native speakers to make the correct choices and they used more implicit knowledge in the process of article selection. This unconscious and effortless acquisition is what Hewson (1972) called "psychomechanism". By contrast, L2 learners have great difficulties acquiring article systems in their second language. Acquiring English articles is a challenge due to the complexity of the English article system.

The French learner and the Spanish learner whose native languages have an article system had a much better performance than Chinese-speaking learners whose native language has no article system. Both of them compared the article structures in English with those in their native languages, which was more frequent than that of the Chinese learner. In other words, language transfer was exhibited in their processing of the passage. Generally speaking, French and Spanish are more marked than English in article system and it explains why the French and the Spanish learner had better performance than the Chinese learner. However, there are some differences in some particular aspect which contributed to the difficulty for them to acquire English articles to be target-like.

The Chinese learner failed to correctly detect SR and HK to decide which article to use. One reason was that the Chinese learner transferred her own knowledge of native language to the target language and failed to correctly perceive definiteness and specificity. Another reason was that the Chinese learner tended to depend heavily on structural rules rather than the dynamic contexts. Her understanding of the articles was totally learned from their teachers' instruction or what she had learned from textbooks. Therefore, she lacked the understanding of the dynamic context of NPs through which the SR and HK could affect the appropriate selection of articles. The Chinese learner had not developed a clear concept of the referential meanings of NPs and that is the reason why she failed to successfully acquire the English article system.

The choices made by the Chinese learner tended to be strongly affected by the rules that she had been taught in class. In other words, she depended heavily on the grammar she had learned. The Chinese learner could not, in some instances, articulate any metalinguistic explanation except for the grammatical rules that she had learned from class instruction. The grammatical rules that were frequently mentioned by the Chinese learner included the following:

(1) *The* should be used when a substance is unique.

(2) *A* or *an* needs to be used when a nominal is introduced for the first time, but when it is mentioned for the second time, *the* should be used.

(3) There should be the definite article *the* in front of musical instruments, but there is no article in front of sports items.

These rules are instructed and drilled over and over again without the learners having a clear idea of how the referential meanings of NPs in the target language are connected with the actual references and how the specificity and definiteness are related to each other. In this way, rule-learning in language acquisition makes language learners assume that there is strong connection between the specific reference and *the* and between a singular countable noun phrase and the indefinite article *a*. Consequently, the Chinese learner failed to perceive the factors of referentiality or specificity and showed confusion when she had to make a choice. Furthermore, the rules can not provide an overall and a coherent view of the English article system and there are a lot of exceptions. It is not easy for language learners to memorize all the rules and exceptions, especially for those whose native languages have no articles.

In addition to the obscure notion of referentiality, the Chinese learner also had a wrong and fixed notion of countability. She tended to think that the countability of the NPs was a fixed or static entity. The data gathered from the tests and interviews show that the Chinese learner decided whether the nouns were countable or uncountable based on her memory. Every time she came across a NP, She tended to refer to her memory to decide to which group the noun belonged. If the noun was not retrievable from memory, she would be confused. The failure for the Chinese learner to perceive the countability of NPs comes from the fact that many English nouns are either countable or uncountable according to different contexts. Wierzbicka (1988: 507) notes that "the fact that many words can be used as either countable or uncountable, depending on the meaning intended, shows that the grammatical characteristics in question are sensitive to changes in the conceptualization". That is to say, the countability judgment should be based on the "conceptualization" of the speakers. Therefore, the proper use of articles also depends on proper conceptualization of the NPs according to the context of the NPs beyond the lexical level.

The patterns for the reasons behind article choices demonstrated by the Chinese learner in present study are similar to Butler's (2002) and Lee's (2013) findings. Butler (2002) found in his study that the learners at lower proficiency levels were heavily influenced by textbooks and teachers' input. They applied the rules separately, ignoring how hearer's knowledge, countability and other contextual factors were related to the selection of articles. Lee (2013: 275) also reported that the beginners in his study "did not express hypotheses related to discourse factors and rather relied on context-insensitive hypotheses influenced by textbook rules". In sum, the Chinese learner depended heavily on some grammatical rules that she had been taught through classroom instruction. She lacked the dynamic perception of SR, HK, and countability, which influenced her proper selection of articles.

The third question concerns how language transfer and markedness affect language learners' perception of article selection and whether they are correlated with each other in a systematic way. It was found that language transfer happened when the target language was more marked than the language learners' native language and unmarked items in their native language were transferred in article selection. It was also found that the L2 learners' confidence was not always consistent with the actual accuracy and the main reason was the correlation of language transfer and markedness. The confidence of the learners came from the similarities between their native languages and the target language as well as their memory of the grammatical rules. The accuracy, however, was based on the markedness degree between the target language and the native language. The high error rate of the indefinite article *a* indicates more difficulty to measure the degree of markedness. As is mentioned above, the French speaker failed to detect that the indefinite article *an* should be used when a word starts with a vowel and made the wrong choice. When he stated the reason for his choice, he made the same mistake, using *a* before the word *hour*. It supports the prediction of Eckman that the relative degree of learning difficulty corresponds to the relative degree of the markedness and suggests that the correlation between language transfer and markedness in article acquisition is systematic.

In sum, language transfer and markedness play a great role in language learners' intuition to acquire English articles. With the experimental analyses, we may have a better understanding of the nature of L2 learners' problems with articles, which can lay a good foundation for addressing the problems of article acquisition.

Chapter 7 General Discussion and Conclusion

This chapter first summarizes the major results and findings from the previous experiments and the interviews. It then offers some possible theoretical and pedagogical implications of this book, the limitations of the present study, as well as the suggestions for future research.

7.1 Major Findings

The present study explores the learners' acquisition of the article system from the perspective of language transfer and markedness theory. It poses three research questions concerning when and how language transfer and markedness function in the process of article acquisition as well as the psychological process of language transfer.

Two experiments and a series of interviews were conducted to answer the questions. A multiple-choice task and a blank-filling task were designed to explore when and how language transfer and markedness function in the process of article acquisition. Statistical analyses were conducted to explore the differences between the [+ART] group and the [−ART] group and the differences between four semantic types of articles. The semi-structured interviews attempted to address the third research question. Through the analyses of the reasons for the learners to choose the answers, the author explored the learners' intuitive perception of language transfer and markedness. The major findings of the present study are as follows:

(1) The unmarked items in language learners' native language will be transferred in the process of article acquisition. The results in Experiment 1 revealed significant difference between Spanish and French L2 learners whose native languages have article system and Chinese L2 learners whose native language does not. It was found that the scores of the [+ART] group learners were higher than those of the [−ART] group. Such difference in accuracy was closely related to the typological differences across languages, particularly the semantic features of noun phrases. Spanish and French are similar to English in terms of semantic and syntactic structures in article system. However, Spanish and French are more marked in gender and number than English. The English noun phrases are only morphologically marked in the feature of number, whereas Chinese has none of the features. Chinese learners tended to transfer the unmarked forms in their native language to the target language, namely, English. That explains why the accuracy of the [+ART] group L2 learners was higher than the [−ART] group. Moreover, the high error rate of *the* in the semantic type of [−SR][+HK] also demonstrates that when

the target language is different from and more marked than native language, it will be difficult for the language learners to acquire. It confirms the first prediction of Markedness Differential Hypothesis (MDH) proposed by Eckman (1977).

(2) The markedness degree between the target language and the native language will affect the difficulty of acquiring the English article system. The high error rate of the indefinite article *an* indicates more difficulty to measure the degree of markedness. The standard of distinguishing *a* and *an* in English is based on whether the following word begins with a vowel, but the standard of distinguishing indefinite articles in French and Spanish depends on gender and number. The difficulty to compare the markedness caused more difficulty for French and Spanish L2 learners to acquire the indefinite article *an*. Therefore, the relative degree of difficulty of comparing markedness is closely related to the corresponding difficulty of acquisition. This finding is consistent with the second prediction of Eckman's MDH.

(3) The psychological process of language transfer from the perspective of markedness is selective and systematic in the process of article acquisition. The further categorization of the learners' response to the interviews proves that they had intuitive perceptions of their native languages. It is the reason why some native language features were transferred into the second language. This conclusion is supported by the fact that French and Spanish L2 learners tended to overuse the definite article in the context of [－SR][＋HK] and the fact that Chinese L2 learners used indefinite article *a* in the context of [－SR]

[−HK] more accurately than the other semantic types.

This book investigates the transferability of the native language from the perspective of markedness degree in the process of article acquisition. It explores the language transfer linguistically and psychologically. A general conclusion can be reached according to the major findings in the study: the English articles can be explained and taught within the framework of markedness. This framework centers on the semantic features of definiteness, specificity of NPs and typological differences of degree of markedness to investigate the usage of articles, which helps us to gain an insight into how to acquire the article system properly.

7.2 Implications

7.2.1 Theoretical Implications

The theoretical implication of the present study lies in the transferability of article system from the perspective of markedness. Empirical research (Master, 1988, 1990, 2002; Zobl, 1983; Kellerman, 1977, 1979, 1986) proves that transferability is constrained by different factors. Ellis (1999) summarizes six constraints that affect transferability and one of them is markedness. The present study investigates the article acquisition from the perspective of language transfer and markedness. The previous syntactic or semantic comparison based on Contrastive Analysis Hypothesis (CAH) claims that all the learning difficulties can be attributed to the differences between the target language and the learner's native language. CAH attributes all the learning difficulties in the interlanguage to the differences between the target language and the learners' native languages, thus putting forward the hypothesis of "difference=difficulty". CAH focuses on the negative transfer of learners' native languages. However, it can not explain why some differences between target language and the learners' native languages will not lead to the learning difficulties among language learners. This study explores the article acquisition from the perspective of markedness and language transfer. The findings signify the possibility of language transfer and examination of learning difficulty through analyzing the degree of markedness.

What's more, a psychological analysis of markedness and language transfer in article acquisition is also employed in this study. Kellerman (1979) claimed that language learners all possess psychotypology, the learners' perceptions about language distance which, together with prototypicality, exert impacts and constraints on transferability. The researchers (H. Mizuno, 1985; M. Mizuno, 1999; Butler, 2002) study the article acquisition from the perspective of psychology, and they mainly focus on the interlanguage development, and the subjects are all Japanese. The present study selects subjects with different native backgrounds and employs a series of semi-structured interviews to examine the perception of the learners when they are making the choice. It is found that the psychological process of transferability from the perspective of markedness is selective and systematic in article acquisition. It provides a new way to investigate the article acquisition.

7.2.2 Pedagogical Implications

Eckman (1985) summarizes two important implications for second language pedagogy which concern the teaching of target language structures in which a markedness relationship exists. "The first is the prediction that the natural order of acquisition follows the degree of markedness of the structures in acquisition; and the second is the direction of generalization of learning from more marked structures to less marked structures." (Eckman, 1985: 290) The first implication is based on the assumption that L2 learners acquire the target structures in an untutored situation. L2 learners tend to acquire relatively less complex structures than those more complex ones. Therefore, they should follow the natural order of acquisition and should be presented with less marked structures before marked ones.

The findings of the present study support the second implication mentioned by Eckman. Strictly speaking, the classroom teaching in China is the foreign language teaching which is different from the untutored acquisition. Therefore, the second implication of Eckman (1985) is suitable for the teaching of the English article system in China. It is a comparatively new way for the teachers to identify and understand the language learners' problems as well as the areas where the language instruction can be made effectively. Eckman claims that "once the most marked member of the set of structures is learned, the learner will be able to generalize to the less marked structures automatically. In other words, if the learner acquires the structure which are most marked, all relatively less marked structures will be learned immediately" (Eckman, 1985: 296). As unmarked forms of the target language appear more frequently than marked ones, it is necessary to increase the input frequency of marked forms in foreign language teaching to overcome the learning difficulties. It requires the teachers in classroom instruction to be equipped with specific knowledge of markedness, aiming to provide more appropriate examples to increase the input frequency of marked forms in the article system.

The in-class instruction can follow the implication of beginning with the more marked structures from two perspectives: First, it can be applied in the intralinguistic comparison of markedness in article system. In classroom instruction, the teachers can teach students to distinguish between marked and unmarked articles. The teaching can start with complex, irregular articles, followed by simpler, more common ones and those with higher frequency. In other words, more marked forms should be taught before the less marked ones. For instance, of the two indefinite articles, *an* is more marked than *a*, and *a* is more common and unmarked. Therefore, *an* should be taught earlier than *a*. Once *an* is acquired, *a* will not be difficult for the learners any more.

Second, teaching more marked forms first can also be applied to the cross-linguistic comparative analysis between English and Chinese NPs. The teachers can apply the typological knowledge to distinguishing the semantic and syntactic structures between English and Chinese NPs. They can teach students to identify marked forms and unmarked ones through comparison. For instance, the semantic functions of indefinite article *a/an* in [−SR][−HK] context are similar to Chinese numeral *yi* (meaning one), but the former can also be used in the context of [−SR][+HK]. When teaching the semantic functions of articles, the teachers can start from the usage of *a/an* in the context of [−SR][+HK] which is more marked and different from the use of Chinese numeral *yi*. If the comparatively more difficult structure of *a/an* in [−SR][+HK] has been acquired, it will be natural for learners to acquire the easier use of *a/an* in [−SR][−HK].

Tomasello and Herron (1988, 1989) point out that the language learners can learn more about the target language when the influence of their native language is openly discussed in class and it is better than focusing on the rote memorization of the target language rules. Frankenberg-Garcia (2000a) also claims through his experimental research that the comparative instruction focusing on the cross-linguistic influence will promote the second language learning. The findings of this research are theoretically and pedagogically significant in that they can help us to explain and predict, to some extent, the difficulties that the Chinese learners come across in the process of acquiring the English article system.

7.3 Limitations and Suggestions for Future Research

Although this study intends to offer a clearer picture of the acquisition of the English article system, it certainly has some limitations. First, only 43 subjects were recruited in the study, which weakens generalizability of the findings. The subjects of the present study are international students in a college in the UK with four different language backgrounds. It facilitates the comparison between the native speakers and nonnative speakers, the [+ART] group L2 learners and [−ART] group L2 learners. However, it is not easy to recruit enough subjects with different native backgrounds, which affects the generalizability of the present study. In future studies it is advisable to probe into the acquisition of article system by collecting samples from different universities.

A second limitation comes from the identification of the semantic types of the NPs. The distinctions of semantic types are sometimes very difficult and the decision to classify the articles and determiners has to be made based on the author's understanding and the surrounding context. In practice, interpreting the NP environment where articles and determiners are used can sometimes differ even among native speakers. Therefore, it is likely that the identification of some classifications of NP contexts in the experiments might need alternative interpretations.

A third limitation lies in the lack of different language

proficiency levels. The subjects in present study belong to the intermediate level, and whether the transferability of native language and markedness manifest the same result in article acquisition among the advanced learners and the beginners needs to be further investigated. The proficiency level of the learners should be more rigidly controlled in future research to examine the relationship between the proficiency of learners and transferability in the process of article acquisition.

Despite the methodological limitations of this study, it is hoped that the findings reported in this study may provide teachers and researchers with a new way of identifying and understanding learners' problems and demonstrate how language instruction can be made more effectively. The findings of this study also indicate the significance of searching a more effective way of teaching the English article system. It may include helping students to overcome some specific kinds of difficulties they commonly come across. This book is a prelude to future research and hopefully, the findings of this study may lay a solid foundation for future research.

Appendix A The Multiple-choice Task

Directions: In this section, you are required to choose the best answer.

1. Let's go to ________ cinema—that'll take your mind off the problem for a while.

A. a B. an C. the D. ∅

2. I looked under ________ bed and found ________ book I lost last week.

A. the; a B. the; the

C. ∅; the D. the; ∅

3. I can't remember when exactly the Robinsons left ________ city. I only remember it was a Monday.

A. a B. an C. the D. ∅

4. I have a beautiful wallet, but ________ wallet was stolen yesterday.

A. a B. an C. the D. ∅

5. Uncle Wang bought a new motor-cycle yesterday. ________ motor-cycle cost him a lot of money.

A. A B. An C. The D. ∅

6. Everywhere man has cut down forests in order to grow crops, or to use ________ wood as fuel or as building material.

A. a B. an C. the D. ∅

7. There are over 58, 000 rocky objects in space, about 900 of which could fall down onto ________ earth.

A. a B. an C. the D. ∅

8. We have every reason to believe that ________ 2008 Beijing Olympic Games will be a success.

A. a B. an C. the D. ∅

9. Scientists have many theories about how ________ universe came into being.

A. a B. an C. the D. ∅

10. Judging from ________ look on his face, he must have news of great excitement to tell us.

A. a B. an C. the D. ∅

11. He smiled ironically in spite of himself, his eyes still fixed in a rather blank stare on ________ young man with the red face.

A. a B. an C. the D. ∅

12. ________ man standing over there is the very man that we have been talking about.

A. A B. An C. The D. ∅

13. Tianan Men Square and ________ Great Wall are tow of the places everyone should see in ________ People's Republic of China.

A. the; the B. ∅; ∅

C. the; ∅ D. ∅; the

14. The foreign tourists marvel at the fine view of ________ West Lake.

A. a　　B. an　　C. the　　D. ∅

15. ________ Wilsons live in an A-shaped house near the coast. It is a 17th century cottage.

A. A　　B. An　　C. The　　D. ∅

16. By nine o'clock, all the Olympic torch bearers had reached the top of ________ Mount Qomolangma on which appeared a rare rainbow soon.

A. a　　B. an　　C. the　　D. ∅

17. ________ Boxing Day, when Christmas boxes used to be given to servants, is the day following ________ Christmas Day.

A. The; the　　B. ∅; ∅

C. The; a　　D. ∅; the

18. In 1864, Lincoln was elected ________ President of the United States for the second time.

A. a　　B. an　　C. the　　D. ∅

19. The salesman showed her several bags and she chose ________ least expensive one as she didn't want to spend too much money on it. Of the two shirts, I'd like to choose ________ less expensive one.

A. a; the　　B. the; the

C. the; a　　D. the; ∅

20. How beautifully she sings! I have never heard ________.

A. the better voice　　B. a good voice

C. the best voice　　D. a better voice

21. Boris has brains. In fact, I doubt whether anyone in the class has ________ IQ.

A. a high　　B. a higher

C. the higher　　D. the highest

22. The warmth of ________ sweater will of course be determined by the sort of wool used.

A. a　　B. an　　C. the　　D. ∅

23. In China, ________ bicycle is a popular means of transportation.

A. a　　B. an　　C. the　　D. ∅

24. I know you don't like ________ music very much. But what do you think of the music in the film we saw yesterday?

A. a　　B. an　　C. the　　D. ∅

25. We wonder what it feels like to be one of ________ really rich. The Smiths already have two Rolls Royce and they are going to buy a third.

A. a　　B. an　　C. the　　D. ∅

26. Bethune then led Wang through the houses where ________ wounded were quartered.

A. a　　B. an　　C. the　　D. ∅

27. Let us get down to fundamentals and agree that ________ young are after all human beings—people just like their elders.

A. a　　B. an　　C. the　　D. ∅

28. Jumping out of ________ airplane at ten thousand feet is quite ________ exciting experience.

A. ∅; the　　B. ∅; an

C. an; an　　D. the; the

29. I was born in New Orleans, Louisiana, ________ city whose name will create a picture of beautiful trees and green grass in our mind.

A. a B. an C. the D. ∅

30. Those successful deaf dancers think that dancing is ________ activity where sight matters more than hearing.

A. a B. an C. the D. ∅

31. I ate ________ sandwich while I was waiting for the 20:08 train.

A. a B. an C. the D. ∅

32. Eric received training in computer for one year, after which he found ________ job in a big company.

A. a B. an C. the D. ∅

33. The man pulled out ________ gold watch, the hands of which were made of small diamonds.

A. a B. an C. the D. ∅

34. Around 1.1 billion people globally do not have ________ access to improved water supply sources.

A. a B. an C. the D. ∅

35. There is ________ "h" in the word "honest".

A. a B. an C. the D. ∅

36. Just because there is ________ ambiguity here, the application still shouldn't ask the user.

A. a B. an C. the D. ∅

37. When he left college, he got a job as ________ reporter in a newspaper office.

A. a B. an C. the D. ∅

38. I earn 10 dollars an hour as ________ supermarket cashier on Saturdays.

A. a B. an C. the D. ∅

39. Mrs Smith told us that they are ________ teachers, not ________ students.

A. the; the B. ∅; ∅

C. the; ∅ D. ∅; the

40. His mother taught ________ piano, but his father was only a blue-collar worker.

A. a B. an C. the D. ∅

41. She always plays ________ football after school.

A. a B. an C. the D. ∅

42. Some of his friends said he could not play ________ violin very well. He was too restless, and travelled around too much.

A. a B. an C. the D. ∅

43. The rice cost one dollar ________ pound.

A. a B. an C. the D. ∅

44. The train is running fifty miles ________ hour.

A. one B. an C. the D. a

45. Eleanor has a thousand pound ________ year entirely at her own disposal.

A. a B. an C. the D. ∅

Appendix B The Blank-filling Task

Directions: In this section, you are required to complete the passage by filling in the blanks with proper determiners.

Science can't explain (1) ________ power of (2) ________ pets, but (3) ________ studies have shown that (4) ________ company of pets can help lower (5) ________ blood pressure and raise (6) ________ chances of recovering from (7) ________ heart attack, reduce (8) ________ loneliness and spread all-round good cheer.

(9) ________ owner will tell you (10) ________ joy (11) ________ pet brings. For some, (12) ________ animal provides (13) ________ comfort than (14) ________ husband/wife. (15) ________ 2002 study by Karen Allen of (16) ________ State University of (17) ________ New York measured (18) ________ stress levels and (19) ________ blood pressure in (20) ________ people—half of them (21) ________ pet owners—while they performed 5 minutes of (22) ________ mental arithmetic or held (23) ________ hand in (24) ________ ice water. (25) ________ subjects completed (26) ________ tasks alone, with (27) ________ husband/wife, (28) ________ close friend or with (29) ________ pet. (30) ________ people with (31) ________ pets did

it best. Those tested with (32) ________ animal friends had smaller change in (33) ________ blood pressure and returned most quickly to (34) ________ baseline heart rates. With (35) ________ pets in (36) ________ room, people also made (37) ________ math mistakes than when doing in front of (38) ________ companions. It seems (39) ________ people feel more released around (40) ________ pets, says Allen, who thinks it may be because (41) ________ pets don't judge.

(42) ________ study reported last fall suggests that having (43) ________ pet dog not only raises (44) ________ spirits but may also have (45) ________ effect on (46) ________ eating habits. (47) ________ researchers at Northwestern Memorial Hospital spent (48) ________ year studying 36 fat people and were put on (49) ________ diet-and-exercise program; (50) ________ separate group of 56 fat people without (51) ________ pets were put on(52) ________ diet program. On average, people lost about 11 pounds, or 5% of (53) ________ body weight. (54) ________ dogs did even better, losing (55) ________ average of 12 pounds, more than 15% of (56) ________ body weight. Dog owners didn't lose any more weight than (57) ________ ones without dogs but, say (58) ________ researchers, got more exercise overall—mostly with (59) ________ dogs—and found it worth doing.

Appendix C Transcription Notation

Symbol	Significance
//	Final fall
/	Slight final fall indicating temporary closure
?	Final rise
,	Slight rise as in listing intonation
-	Truncation (e. g. , what ti-what time is it/)
_	Level ending
..	Pauses of less than 0. 5 second
...	Pauses greater than 0. 5 second (unless precisely timed)
⟨2⟩	Precise units of time (=2 second pause)
=	To indicate overlap and latching of speakers' utterances' spacing and single= before and after the appropriate portions of the text to indicate overlap; turn-initial double = to indicate latching of the utterance to the preceding one. E. g. R: so you understand =the requirements? = B: =yeah, i understand them/= ---------- R: so you understand the requirements? B: = =yeah, i understand them/
::	Lengthened segments (e. g. , wha::t)

~	Fluctuating intonation over one word
*	Accent; normal prominence
* *	Extra prominence
{{ }}	Nonlexical phenomena, both vocal and nonvocal, that overlay the lexical stretch (e. g. , {{lo}}text//)
[ ]	Nonlexical phenomena, both vocal and nonvocal, that interrupt the lexical stretch (e. g. , text [laugh]text//)
( )	Unintelligible speech
di(d)	A good guess at an unclear segment
(did)	A good guess at an unclear word
(xxx)	Unclear word for which a good guess can be made as to how many syllables were uttered, with each x equal to one syllable
(" ")	Regularization (e. g. , i'm gonna ("going to")come soon/)
# #	Use cross-hatches when extratextual information needs to be included within the text (e. g. , R: did you ask M #surname# to come?)

(Allwright and Bailey, 1991)

Bibliography

Aarts, J. and F. Aarts. *English Syntactic Structures: Functions and Categories in Sentence Analysis*. New York: Prentice Hall, 1988.

Abney, S. P. The English noun phrase in its sentential aspect. Ph. D. Dissertation. MIT, Cambridge MA, 1987.

Abrahamsson, N. Vowel epenthesis of /sC (C)/ onsets in Spanish/Swedish interphonology: A longitudinal case study. *Language Learning*, 1999(49), pp. 473-508.

Alenizi, A. M. The acquisition of the nongeneric uses of the English definite article the by Arabic speakers of English. M. A. Dissertation. Southern Illinois University Carbondale, 2013.

Al-Jarrah, M. The transfer of Arabic rhetorical patterns into Jordanian students' writing in English. *Mu'tah Lil-Buhūth Wad-Dirāsāt: Humanities and Social Sciences Series*, 2001, 16(8), pp. 223-246.

Allwright, R. and K. Bailey. *Focus on the Language Classroom*. Cambridge: Cambridge University Press, 1991.

Anderson, J. The markedness differential hypothesis and syllable structure difficulty. In G. Ioup and S. Weinberger (eds.), *Interlanguage Phonology: The Acquisition of a*

Second *Language Sound System*. Cambridge, MA: Newbury House, 1987, pp. 277-291.

Angelis, G. and L. Selinker. Interlanguage transfer and competing linguistic systems in the multilingual mind. In J. Cenoz (ed.), *Cross-linguistic Influence in Third Language Acquisition: Psycholinguistic Perspectives*. Clevedon, England: Multilingual Matters, 2001, pp. 8-20.

Anthony, P. *Translation and Text Transfer—An Essay on the Principles of Intercultural Communication*. Tarragona: Intercultural Studies Group, 2010.

Ashild, N. What markedness marks: The markedness problem with direct objects. *Lingua*, 2004, 114 (9/10), pp. 1186-1212.

Bailey, N., C. Madden and S. Krashen. Is there a "natural sequence" in adult second language learning? *Language Learning*, 1974 (24), pp. 235-243.

Bartlet, H. G. Rhetorical redundancy in Apachean English interlanguage. *Research on Language and Social Interaction*, 1980 (13), pp. 689-704.

Bartlet, H. G. Transfer and variability of rhetorical redundancy in Apachean English Interlanguage. In S. Gass and L. Selinker (eds.), *Language Transfer in Language Transfer Learning*. Rowley, MA: Newbury House, 1983, pp. 279-305.

Battistella, E. L. *Markedness—The Evaluative Superstructure of Language*. Albany, NY: State University of New York Press, 1990.

Berry, R. *Articles*. London: HarperCollins, 1993.

Biber, D. and R. Conrad. *Corpus Linguistics*. Beijing: Foreign Language Teaching and Research Press, 2000.

Bickerton, D. *Roots of Language*. Ann Arbor: Karoma, 1981.

Bresson, F. Remarks on genetic psycholinguistics: The acquisition of the article system in French. *Problems Actuels en Psycholinguistique*. Paris: Centre Nationale de la Recherche Scientifique, 1974, pp. 67-72.

Brown, R. *A First Language: The Early Stages*. Cambridge, MA: Harvard University Press, 1973.

Butler, G. Second language learners' theories on the use of English articles, an analysis of the metalinguistic knowledge used by Japanese students in acquiring the English article system. *Studies in Second Language Acquisition*, 2002 (24), pp. 451-480.

Cardoso, W. The variable development of English word-final stops by Brazilian Portuguese speakers: A stochastic optimality theoretic account. *Language Variation and Change*, 2007 (19), pp. 1-30.

Carlisle, R. Environment and markedness as interacting constraints on vowel epenthesis. In W. Strange (ed.), *Speech Perception and Linguistic Experience: Issues in Cross-language Research*. Baltimore: York Press, 1992, pp. 171-204.

Cenoz, J. The effect of linguistic distance, L2 status, and age on cross-linguistic influence in third language acquisition. In J. Cenoz (ed.), *Cross-linguistic Influence in Third Language Acquisition: Psycholinguistic Perspectives*. Clevedon, England: Multilingual Matters, 2001, pp. 8-20.

Chen, P. Identifiability and definiteness in Chinese. *Linguistics*, 2004, 42(6), pp. 1129-1184.

Cheng, L. and R. Sybesma. Bare and not-so-bare nouns and the structure of NP. *Linguistic Inquiry*, 1999, 30(4), pp. 509-542.

Chesterman, A. *On Definiteness: A Study with a Special Reference to English and Finnish*. New York: Cambridge University Press, 1991.

Chierchia, G. Reference to kinds across language. *Natural Language Semantics*, 1998 (6), pp. 339-405.

Chomsky, N. A review of B. F. Skinner's verbal behavior. *Language*, 1959(35), pp. 26-58.

Chomsky, N. *Lectures on Government and Binding*. Dordrecht: Foris, 1981.

Chomsky, N. *Knowledge of Language*. New York: Praeger, 1986.

Christopherson, P. *The Articles: A Study of Their Theory and Use in English*. Munksgaard, Copenhagen, 1939.

Clahsen, H., J. Meisel and M. Pienemann. *Deutsch als Zweitsprache: Der Spracherwerb Auslandischer Arbeiter*. Tubingen: Narr, 1983.

Connor, U. *Contrastive Rhetoric: Cross-cultural Aspects of Second-language Writing*. New York: Cambridge University Press, 1996.

Corder, S. Idiosyncratic dialects and error analysis. *International Review of Applied Linguistics*, 1971(V), pp. 149-159.

Corder, S. *Error Analysis and Interlanguage*. Oxford: Oxford University Press, 1981.

Croft, W. *Typology and Universals*. Cambridge: Cambridge University Press, 1990.

Crompton, P. Article errors in the English writing of advanced L1 Arabic learners: The role of transfer. *Asian EFL Journal, Professional Teaching Articles*, 2011 (50), pp. 4-35.

Cummins, J. *Interdependence and Bicultural Ambivalence: Regarding the Pedagogical Rationale for Bilingual Education*. Arlington: National Clearinghouse for Bilingual Education, 1982.

Cummins, J. *Language, Power, and Pedagogy: Bilingual Children in the Crossfire*. Clevedon: Multilingual Matters, 2000.

Dakin, J. *The Language Laboratory and Language Learning*. London, Longman, 1973.

De Angelis, G. and L. Selinker. Interlanguage transfer and competing linguistic systems in the multilingual mind. In J. Cenoz (ed.), *Cross-linguistic Influence in Third Language Acquisition: Psycholinguistic Perspectives*. Clevedon, England: Multilingual Matters, 2001, pp. 42-58.

De Jong, K., N. H. Silbert and H. Park. Generalization across segments in second language consonant identification. *Language Learning*, 2009(59), pp. 1-31.

Dekydtspotter, L., B. D. Schwartz and R. A. Sprouse. The comparative fallacy in L2 processing research. In M. G. O'Brien, C. Shea and J. Archibald (eds.), *Proceedings of the 8th Generative Approaches to Second Language Acquisition Conference (GASLA 2006)*. Somerville, MA:

Cascadilla Proceedings Project, 2006, pp. 33-40.

Diesing, M. *Indefiniteness*. Cambridge, MA: MIT Press, 1992.

Dulay, H. and M. Burt. Errors and strategies and child second language acquisition. *TESOL Quarterly*, 1974a (8), pp. 129-136.

Dulay, H. and M. Burt. Natural sequences in child second language acquisition. *Language Learning*, 1974b (24), pp. 37-53.

Dulay, H. and M. Burt. A new approach to discovering universal strategies of child second language acquisition. In D. P. Dato (ed.), *Developmental Psycholinguistics: Theory and Applications*. Washington, D. C.: Georgetown University Press, 1975, pp. 209-233.

Dulay, H. and M. Burt. Remarks on creativity in language acquisition. In M. Burt, H. Dulay and M. Finnochiaro (eds.), *Viewpoints on English as a Second Language*. New York: Regents, 1977, pp. 95-126.

Eckman, F. Markedness and the Contrastive Analysis Hypothesis. *Language Learning*, 1977, 27 (2), pp. 315-330.

Eckman, F. Some theoretical and pedagogical implications of Markedness Differential Hypothesis. *Studies in Second Language Acquisition*, 1985, 7(3), pp. 289-307.

Eckman, F. The markedness differential hypothesis: Theory and applications. In B. Wheatley, A. Hastings, F. Eckman et al. (eds.), *Current Approaches to Second Language Acquisition: Proceedings of the 1984 University of Wisconsin-Milwaukee Linguistics Symposium*. Indiana University Linguistics Club Bloomingtonn Milwaukee,

1985, pp. 3-21.

Eckman, F. Second language phonology. In S. Gassand and A. Mckey (eds.), *The Routledge Handbook of Second Language Acquisition*. Milton Park, Abingdon, 2012, pp. 91-105.

Ellis, R. *The Study of Second Language Acquisition*. Oxford: Oxford University Press, 1994.

Ellis, R. *The Study of Second Language Acquisition*. Shanghai: Shanghai Foreign Language Education Press, 1999.

Ellis, N. C. Selective attention and transfer phenomena in L2 acquisition: Contingency, cue competition, salience, interference, overshadowing, blocking, and perceptual learning. *Applied Linguistics*, 2006 (27), pp. 164-194.

Epstein, S., S. Flynn and G. Martohardjono. Second language acquisition: Theoretical and experimental issues in contemporary research. *Behavioral and Brain Sciences*, 1996 (19), pp. 677-738.

Fakhri, A. *Text Organization and Transfer*. IRAL, XXXII. 1, 1994.

Flynn, S. *A Parameter-setting Model of L2 Acquisition*. Dordrecht: Reidel, 1987.

Fodor, J. and I. Sag. Referential and quantificational indefinites. *Linguistics and Philosophy*, 1982(5), pp. 355-398.

Franceschina, F. Morphological or syntactic deficits in near-native speakers? An assessment of some current proposals. *Second Language Research*, 2001(17), pp. 213-247.

Frankenberg-Garcia, A. Using a translation corpus to teach

English to native speakers of Portuguese. *A Journal of Anglo-American Studies*, 2000a (3), pp. 65-78.

Fries, C. *Teaching and Learning English as a Foreign Language*. Ann Arbor: University of Chicago Press, 1945.

Garton, A. An approach to the study of determiners in early language development. *Journal of Psycholinguistic Research*, 1983, 12(5), pp. 13-525.

Gass, S. Language transfer and universal grammatical relations. *Language Learning*, 1979(29), pp. 327-344.

Gass, S. Language transfer and universal grammatical relations. In S. Gass and L. Selinker (eds.), *Language Transfer in Language Learning*. Rowley, MA: Newbury House, 1983, pp. 69-82.

Gass, S. Second language acquisition and linguistic theory: The role of language transfer. In S. Flynn (ed.), *Linguistic Theory in Second Language Acquisition*. Kluwer Academic Publisher, 1988, pp. 384-403.

Gass, S. and L. Selinker. *Language Transfer in Language Learning*. Amsterdam/Philadelphia: John Benjamins, 1992.

Gilbert, G. Transfer in second language acquisition. In R. W. Andersen (ed.), *Pidginization and Creolization as Language Acquisitio*n. Rowley, MA: Newbury House, 1983, pp. 168-181.

Givon, T. *Syntax* (Vol. II). Amsterdam: John Benjamins Publishing Company, 1990.

Givon, T. *Dualism and Grammar*. Amsterdam: John Benjamins Publishing Company, 1995.

Goad, H. and L. White. Ultimate attainment of L2 inflections:

Effects of L1 prosodic structure. In S. Foster-Cohen, M. Ota, M. A. Sharwood Smith and A. Sorace (eds.), *EUROSLA Yearbook*. Amsterdam: John Benjamins, 2004, pp. 119-145.

Greenberg, J. H. *Language Universals*. The Hague: Mouton, 1966.

Gundel, J., K. Houlihan and G. Sanders. Markedness distribution in phonology and syntax. In F. Eckman, E. Moravcsik and J. Wirth (eds.), *Markedness*. New York: Plenum Press, 1986, pp. 107-138.

Hackmann, D. Patterns in purported speech acts. *Journal of Pragmatics*, 1977(1), pp. 143-154.

Hammarberg, B. The role of L1 and L2 in L3 production and acquisition. In J. Cenoz (ed.), *Cross-linguistic Influence in Third Language Acquisition: Psycholinguistic Perspectives*. Clevedon, England: Multilingual Matters, 2001, pp. 21-41.

Hawkins, J. A. *Definiteness and Indefiniteness: A Study in Reference and Grammaticality Prediction*. London: Croom Helm Ltd., 1978.

Hawkins, J. A. On (in)definite articles: Implicatures and (un)grammaticality prediction. *Journal of Linguistics*, 1991(27), pp. 405-442.

Hawkins, R. Persistent selective fossilisation in second language acquisition and the optimal design of the language faculty. *Essex Research Reports in Linguistics*, 2000(34), pp. 75-90.

Hawkins, R. *Second Language Syntax: A Generative Introduction*. Oxford: Blackwell, 2001.

Hawkins, R. Representational deficit theories of (adult) SLA: Evidence, counterevidence and implications. Unpublished paper presented at European Second Language Association annual conference (EUROSLA 13), Edinburgh, September, 2003.

Hawkins, R., S. Al-Eid, I. Almahboob, P. Athanasopoulos, R. Chaengchenkit, J. Hu, M. Rezai, C. Jaensch, Y. Jeon, A. Jiang, I. Leung, K. Matsunaga, M. Ortega, G. Sarko, N. Snape and K. Velasco-Zarate. Accounting for English article interpretation by L2 speakers. In S. H. Foster-Cohen (ed.), *EUROSLA Yearbook 6*, 2006, pp. 7-25.

Hawkins, R. and S. Liszka. Locating the source of defective past tense marking in advanced L2 English speakers. In R. van Hout, A. Hulk, F. Kuiken and R. Towell (eds.), *In the Lexicon-Syntax Interface in Second Language Acquisition*. Amsterdam: John Benjamins, 2003, pp. 21-44.

Hawkins, R. and Y. Chan. The partial availability of UG in SLA: The failed functional features hypothesis. *Second Language Research*, 1997, 13(3), pp. 187-226.

Haznedar, B. and B. D. Schwartz. Are there optional infinitives in child L2 acquisition? In E. Hughes, M. Hughes and A. Greenhill (eds.), *Proceedings of the 21st Annual Boston University Conference on Language Development*. Somerville, MA: Cascadilla Press, 1997, pp. 257-268.

Hewson, J. *Article and Noun in English*. The Hague, Mouton, 1972.

Hinds, J. Contrastive rhetoric: Japanese and English. *Text*, 1983(3), pp. 183-195.

Hinds, J. Reader versus writer responsibility: A new typology. In U. Connor and R. B. Kaplan (eds.), *Writing across*

Languages: *Analysis of L2 Text*, *Reading*. MA: Addison-Wesley, 1987, pp. 141-152.

Hirose, K. Comparing L1 and L2 organizational patterns in the argumentative writing of Japanese EFL students' expository writing in English: An exploratory study. *Journal of Second Language Writing*, 2003(3), pp. 203-229.

Hsin, A. On indefinite subject NPs in Chinese. *Chinese Studies* (Hanxueyanjiu), 2002, 20(2), pp. 353-376.

Hsin, A. A preliminary study of acquisition of English DP by Chinese EFL learners in Taiwan. *Taiwan Journal of TESOL*, 2007 (4), pp. 43-66.

Hsu, H. Interaction between markedness and transfer in English coda nasals: Taiwanese learning English as a foreign language. *Studies in Media and Communication*, 2013, 1 (1), pp. 64-90.

Huebner, T. *A Longitudinal Analysis of the Acquisition of English*. Ann Arbor: Karoma, 1983.

Huebner, T. System and variability in interlanguage syntax. *Language Learning*, 1985(35), pp. 141-163.

Hume, E. Markedness. In M. Van Oostendorp, C. Ewen, E. Hume and K. Rice (eds.), *Companion to Phonology*. Blackwell, 2011, pp. 79-106.

Hüseyin, A. Positive transfer samples from the bridge language English in learning and teaching German. *Journal of International Social Research*, 2010, 3(10), pp. 50-60.

Hyltenstam, K. *Variation in Interlanguage Syntax*. Working Papers, 1978.

Hyltenstam, K. The use of typological markedness as a

predictor in second language acquisition: The case of pronominal copies in relative clauses. In R. W. Andersen (ed.), *Second Language: A Crosslinguistic Perspective*. Rowley, MA: Newbury House, 1984, pp. 39-58.

Ionin, T. This is definitely specific: Specificity and definiteness in article systems. *Natural Language Semantics*, 2006 (14), pp. 175-234.

Ionin, T., H. Ko and K. Wexler. Specificity as a grammatical notion: Evidence from L2 English article use. In G. Guarding and M. Tsujimura (eds.), *Proceedings of WCCFL 22*. Somerville. MA: Cascadilla Press, 2003, pp. 245-258.

Ionin, T., H. Ko and K. Wexler. Article semantics in L2-acquisition: The role of specificity. *Language Acquisition*, 2004(12), pp. 2-69.

Ionin, T., S. Back and E. Kim. *That*'s not so different from *the*: Definite and demonstrative descriptions in second language acquisition. *Second Language Research*, 2012, 28 (1), pp. 69-101.

Ionin, T. and S. Montrul. The role of L1 transfer in the interpretation of articles with definite plurals in L2 English. *Language Learning*, 2010, 60(4), pp. 877-925.

Ionin, T., S. Montrul and M. Crivos. A bidirectional study on the acquisition of plural noun phrase interpretation in English and Spanish. *Applied Psycholinguistics*, 2013, 34 (3), pp. 483-518.

Ionin, T., Z. Maria and M. Salvador. Sources of linguistic knowledge in the second language acquisition of English articles. *Lingua*, 2007(118), pp. 554-576.

Isabelli-García, C. and R. Slough. Acquisition of the non-generic definite article by Spanish learners of English as a foreign language. *Onomázein*, 2012(25), pp. 95-105.

Jakobson, R. The structure of the Russian verb. In L. Waugh and M. Halle (eds.), *Russian and Slavic Grammar Studies, 1931-1981*. Berlin etc.: Mouton, 1984a, pp. 1-14.

Jakobson, R. Contributions to the general theory of case: General meanings of the Russian cases. In L. Waugh and M. Halle (eds.), *Russian and Slavic Grammar Studies, 1931-1981*. Berlin etc.: Mouton, 1984b, pp. 59-103.

James, C. *Errors in Language Learning and Use: Exploring Error Analysis*. Essex: Longman, 1998.

Kaplan, R. B. Cultural thought patterns in inter-cultural education. *Language Learning*, 1966(16), pp. 1-20.

Kaplan, R. B. *The Anatomy of Rhetoric: Prolegomena to a Functional Theory of Rhetoric*. Philadelphia: Center for Curriculum Development, 1972.

Kaplan, R. B. Contrastive rhetoric and second language learning: Notes toward a theory of contrastive rhetoric. In A. Purves (ed.), *Writing across Languages and Cultures: Issues in Contrastive Rhetoric*. Newbury Park, CA: Sage, 1988, pp. 275-304.

Kaplan, R. B. Concluding essay: On applied linguistics and discourse analysis. *Annual Review of Applied Linguistics*, 1991 (2), pp. 199-204.

Kaplan, R. B. What in the World is Contrastive Rhetoric? In C.

G. Panetta (ed.), *Contrastive Rhetoric Revisited and Redefined*. Lawrence Erlbaum Associates Publishers, 2001, pp. vii-xx.

Kasper, G. Errors in speech act realization and use of gambits. *The Canadian Modern Language Review*, 1979a (35), pp. 395-406.

Kasper, G. Pragmatische Defizite im Englischen deutscher Lerner. *Linguistik und Didaktik*, 1979b(10), pp. 370-379.

Kasper, G. Pragmatic Transfer. *Second Language Research*, 1992, 8(3), pp. 203-231.

Kellerman, E. Towards a characterization of strategies of transfer in second language learning. *Interlanguage Studies Bulletin*, 1977 (2), pp. 58-145.

Kellerman, E. Transfer and non-transfer: Where are we now? *Studies in Second Language Acquisition*, 1979 (2), pp. 37-57.

Kellerman, E. Now you see it, now you don't. In S. Gass and L. Selinker (eds.), *Language Transfer in Language Learning*. Rowley, MA: Newbury House, 1983, pp. 112-134.

Kellerman, E. An eye for an eye: Crosslinguistic constraints on the development of the L2 Lexicon. In E. Kellerman and M. S. Smith (eds.), *Cross-linguistic Influence in Second Language Acquisition*. Oxford: Pergamon Press Ltd., 1986, pp. 35-48.

Kellerman, E. The imperfect conditional. In K. Hyltenstam and L. K. Obler (eds.), *Bilingualism across the Lifespan*. Cambridge: Cambridge University Press, 1989, pp. 87-115.

Ko, H., A. Perovic, T. Ionin and K. Wexler. Semantic universals and variation in L2 article choice. In R. Slabakova, J. Rothman, P. Kempchinsky, and E. Gavruseva (eds.), *Proceedings of the 9th Generative Approaches to Second Language Acquisition Conference* (*GASLA 9*). Somerville, MA: Cascadilla Proceedings Project, 2008, pp. 118-129.

Ko, H., T. Ionin. and K. Wexler. Adult L2-learners lack the maximality presupposition, too. In K. U. Deen et al. (eds.), *The Proceedings of the Inaugural Conference on Generative Approaches to Language Acquisition—North America, Honolulu, HI*. University of Connecticut Occasional Papers in Linguistics, 2006, pp. 171-182.

Ko, H., T. Ionin. and K. Wexler. The role of presuppositionality in the second language acquisition of English articles. *Linguistic Inquiry*, 2010, 41 (2), pp. 213-254.

Kobayashi, H. and C. Rinnert. Factors affecting composition evaluation in an EFL context: Cultural rhetorical pattern and readers' background. *Language and Learning*, 1996 (46), pp. 397-437.

Kobayashi, H. and C. Rinnert. High school student perceptions of first language literacy instruction: Implications for second language writing. *Journal of Second Language Writing*, 2002, 11(2), pp. 91-116.

Kobayashi, H. and C. Rinnert. Take response and text construction across L1 and L2 writing. *Journal of Second Language Writing*, 2007, 17(1), pp. 7-29.

Kramsky, J. *The Article and the Concept of Definiteness in Language*. The Hague, Mouton, 1972.

Krashen, S. D. *Second Language Acquisition and Second Language Learning*. Oxford, New York: Pergamon Press, 1981.

Krifka, M. Common nouns: A contrastive analysis of Chinese and English. In G. N. Carlson and F. J. Pelletier (eds.), *The Generic Book*. Chicago: Chicago Press, 1995, pp. 398-411.

Kubota, R. Contrastive rhetoric of Japanese and English: A critical approach. Unpublished Ph. D. Dissertation. University of Toronto, 1992.

Kubota, R. and A. Lehner. Toward critical contrastive rhetoric. *Journal of Second Language Writing*, 2004, 13 (1), pp. 7-27.

Kubota, R. and A. Lehner. Response to Ulla Connor's comments. *Journal of Second Language Writing*, 2005, 14(2), pp. 137-143.

Lado, R. *Linguistics across Cultures: Applied Linguistics for Language Teachers*. Ann Arbor: University of Michigan Press, 1957.

Lardiere, D. Some thoughts on the contrastive analysis of features in second language acquisition. *Second Language Research*, 2009, 25(2), pp. 173-227.

Larsen-Freeman, D. An explanation for the morpheme acquisition order of second language learners. *Language Learning*, 1976(25), pp. 125-135.

Larsen-Freeman, D. and M. H. Long. *An Introduction to*

Second Language Acquisition Research. London: Longman, 1991.

Lee, J. A comprehensive study of the use of English articles by Korean L2 speakers of English: Speaking, writing, and metalinguistic awareness. Ph. D. Dissertation. The State University of New Jersey, New Jersey, 2013.

Leech, G. *Semantics*. Harmondsworth: Penguin, 1981.

Leech, G. *Principles of Pragmatics*. London: Longman, 1983.

Li, C. and S. Thompson. *Mandarin Chinese: A Reference Grammar*. Berkeley: University of California University, 1981.

Li, H. Y. and L. R. Yang. An investigation of English articles' acquisition by Chinese learners of English. *Chinese Journal of Applied Linguistics*, 2010, 33(3), pp. 15-31.

Liang, Yu-Chang. Markedness in L1 transfer—L2 acquisition of Mandarin classifiers. Paper presented at the 11th Generative Approaches to Second Language Acquisition, Washington, 2011.

Liu, D. L. and J. L. Gleason. Acquisition of the article "the" by nonnative speakers of English. *Studies in Second Language Acquisition*, 2002(24), pp. 1-26.

Lu, C. and C. Fen. The acquisition of English articles by Chinese learners. *Second Language Studies*. 2001, 20(1), pp. 43-78.

Lyons, C. *Definiteness*. Cambridge: Cambridge University Press, 1999.

Major, R. Markedness in second language acquisition of consonant clusters. *Studies in Second Language*

Acquisition, 1996(18), pp. 69-90.

Master, P. A cross-linguistic interlanguage analysis of the acquisition of the English article system. Ph. D. Dissertation. University of California, Los Angeles, 1987.

Master, P. Acquiring the English article system: A cross-linguistic interlanguage analysis. Paper presented at the 22nd annual TESOL convention 8-13, Chicago, Illinois, 1988.

Master, P. Teaching the English articles as a binary system. *TESOL Quarterly*, 1990, 24(3), pp. 461-478.

Master, P. The English article system: Acquisition, function, and pedagogy. *System*, 1997(25), pp. 215-232.

Master, P. Information structure and English article pedagogy. *System*, 2002(30), pp. 331-348.

Mazurkewich, I. Syntactic markedness and language acquisition. *Studies in Second Language Acquisition*, 1985, 7(1), pp. 15-35.

Mizuno, H. A psycholinguistic approach to the article system in English. *JACET Bulletin*, 1985 (16), pp. 1-29.

Mizuno, M. Interlanguage Analysis of the English Article System: Some Cognitive Constraints Facing the Japanese Adult Learners. *International Review of Applied Linguistics in Language Teaching*, 1999, 37 (2), pp. 127-170.

Muromatsu, K. Classifiers and the count/mass distinction. In Y. H. A. Li and A. Simpson (eds.), *Functional Structure(s), Form and Interpretation: Perspectives from East Asian Languages*. London: Routledge, Curzon, 2003, pp. 65-128.

Nemser, W. Approximative systems of foreign language learners. *International Review of Applied Linguistics*, 1971(IX), pp. 115-123.

Odlin, T. *Language Transfer: Cross-linguistic Influence in Language Learning*. Cambridge, UK: Cambridge University Press, 1989.

Odlin, T. Transferability and Linguistic Substrates. *Second Language Research*, 1992(8), pp. 171-202.

Odlin, T. *Language Transfer, Cross-linguistic Influence in Language Learning*. Shanghai: Shanghai Foreign Language Education Press, 2001.

Ostler, S. E. Contrastive rhetoric: An expanding paradigm. In J. Flowerdew (ed.), *Academic Discourse*. London: Longman, 2001, pp. 167-181.

Parrish, B. A new look at methodologies in the study of article acquisition for learners of ESL. *Language Learning*, 1987 (37), pp. 361-383.

Prévost, P. and L. White. Missing surface inflection or impairment? Evidence from tense and agreement. *Second Language Research*, 2000, 16(2), pp. 103-133.

Quirk, R. *A Grammar of Contemporary English*. London: Longman, 1972.

Radford, A. *Syntactic Theory and the Structure of English*. London: Cambridge University Press, 1997.

Radford, A. *Minimalist Syntax*. Cambridge: CUP, 2006.

Rayson, P., G. Leech and M. Hodges. Social differentiation in the use of English vocabulary. *International Journal of*

Corpus Linguistics, 1997, 2(1), pp. 133-152.

Reid, J., P. Battaglia, M. Schuldt, E. Narita, M. Mochizuki and N. Snape. The article choice of learners of English as a second language. Unpublished term paper, University of Essex, UK. 2006.

Ringbom, H. *Foreign Language Learning and Bilingualism*. Abo Akademi, 1985.

Rivers, W. Contrastive linguistics in textbook and classroom. *English Teaching Forum*, 1970(8), pp. 7-10.

Robertson, D. Variability in the use of the English article system by Chinese learners of English. *Second Language Research*, 2000, 16(2), pp. 135-172.

Rutherford, W. Markedness in second language acquisition. *Language Learning*, 1982(32), pp. 85-108.

Schwartz, B. and R. Sprouse. Word order and nominative case in nonnative language acquisition: A longitudinal study of (L1 Turkish) German interlanguage. In T. Hockstra and B. Schwartz (eds.), *Language Acquisition Studies in Generative Grammar*. Amsterdam: John Benjamins, 1994, pp. 317-368.

Schwartz, B. and R. Sprouse. L2 cognitive states and the full transfer/full access model. *Second Language Research*, 1996(12), pp. 40-72.

Selinker, L. Interlanguage. *International Review of Applied Linguistics*, 1972(X), pp. 209-230.

Sio, J. Modification and reference in the Chinese nominal. Ph. D. Dissertation. University of Leiden, the Netherlands, 2006.

Smith, N. V. and I. M. Tsimpli. *The Mind of a Savant*:

Language Learning and Modularity. Oxford: Blackwell, 1995.

Snape, N. The acquisition of English determiner phrase by Japanese and Spanish learners of English. Ph. D. Dissertation. University of Essex, 2007.

Snape, N., N. Leung and Hui-Chuan Ting. Comparing Chinese, Japanese and Spanish speakers in L2 English article acquisition: Evidence against the Fluctuation Hypothesis? In M. G. O'Brien, C. Shea, and J. Archibald (eds.), *Proceedings of the 8th Generative Approaches to Second Language Acquisition Conference* (*GASLA 2006*). Somerville, MA: Cascadilla Proceedings Project, 2006, pp. 132-139.

Spolsky, B. *Conditions for Second Language Learning*. Oxford: Oxford University Press, 1989.

Stockwell, R., P. Schachter and B. Partee. *The Major Syntactic Structures of English*. New York: Holt, Rinehart and Winston, 1973.

Su, I-Ru. Transfer of pragmatic competences: A bi-directional perspective. *Modern Language Journal*, 2010, 94 (1), pp. 87-102.

Su, I-Ru. Bi-directional transfer in Chinese EFL Learners' apologizing behavior. *Concentric*: *Studies in linguistics*, 2012, 38(2), pp. 237-266.

Tamar, D. Bidirectional transfer: Consequences of translation ambiguity for bilingual word meaning. Ph. D. Dissertation. University of Pittsburgh, 2011.

Tang, Ting-che. *The Collection of Chinese Morphology and*

Syntax Researches (Han-yu ci-fa yu ju-fa lun-ji). Taipei: Student Bookstore, 1988.

Tarone, E. and B. Parrish. Task-related variation in interlanguage: The case of articles. *Language Learning*, 1988 (38), pp. 21-44.

Thomas, G. Mandarin *hen* and universal markedness in gradable adjectives. *Natural Language and Linguistic Theory*, 2012, 30(2), pp. 513-565.

Thomas, M. The acquisition of English articles by first-and second-language learners. *Applied Psycholinguistics*, 1989 (10), pp. 335-355.

Ting, H. C. The acquisition of articles in L2 English by L1 Chinese and L1 Spanish speakers. Unpublished MA Dissertation. University of Essex, UK, 2005.

Tomasello, M. and C. Herron. Down the garden path: Inducing and correcting overgeneralization errors in the foreign language classroom. *Applied Psycholinguistics*, 1988(9), pp. 237-246.

Tomasello, M. and C. Herron. Feedback for language transfer errors: The Garden Path technique. *Studies in Second Language Acquisition*, 1989 (11), pp. 385-395.

Tomioka, S. The semantics of Japanese null pronouns and its cross-linguistic implications. In K. Schwabe and S. Winkler (eds.), *The Interfaces: Deriving and Interpreting Omitted Structures*. Amsterdam: John Benjamins, 2003, pp. 321-334.

Trenkic, D. Variability in L2 article production: Beyond the representational deficit vs. processing constraints debate.

Second Language Research, 2007, 23(3), pp. 289-327.

Trenkic, D. The representation of English articles in second language grammars: Determiners or adjectives? *Bilingualism: Language and Cognition*, 2008(11), pp. 1-18.

Trubetzkoy, N. Phonologie et géographie linguistique. *Travaux du Cercle Linguistique de Prague*, 1931(4), pp. 228-234.

Tryzna, M. Questioning the validity of the Article Choice Parameter and the Fluctuation Hypothesis: Evidence from L2 English article use by L1 Polish and L1 Mandarin Chinese speakers. In G. Mayo, M. del Pilar and R. Hawkins (eds.), *Second Language Acquisition of Articles*, 2009, pp. 67-86.

Vainikka, A. and M. Young-Scholten. Direct access to X'-theory: Evidence from Korean and Turkish adults learning German. In T. Hoekstra and B. D. Schwartz (eds.), *Language Acquisition Studies in Generative Grammar: Papers in Honour of Kenneth Wexler from 1991 GLOW Workshops*. Philadelphia, PA: John Benjamins, 1994, pp. 265-316.

Vainikka, A. and M. Young-Scholten. Gradual development of L2 phrase structure. *Second Language Research*, 1996a (12), pp. 7-39.

Vainikka, A. and M. Young-Scholten. The early stages in adult L2 syntax: Additional evidence from romance speakers. *Second Language Research*, 1996b, 12(12), pp. 140-176.

Wakabayashi, S. The acquisition of functional categories by learners of English. Unpublished Ph. D. Dissertation. University of Cambridge, Cambridge, UK. 1997.

Wakabayashi, S. Systematicity in the use of the definite article by Japanese learners of English. *Gunma kenritsu joshi daigaku kiyo*, 1998 (19), pp. 91-107.

Warden, D. A. The influence of context on Children's use of identifying expressions and references. *British Journal of Psychology*, 1976 (67), pp. 101-102.

Wardhaugh, R. The contrastive analysis hypothesis. *TESOL Quarterly*, 1970, 4(2), pp. 123-130.

Weinreich, U. *Language in Contact: Findings and Problems*. New York: Linguistic Circle of New York, 1953.

White, L. Markedness and parameter setting: Some implications for a theory of adult second language learning. *McGill Working Papers in Linguistics*, 1983(13), pp. 107-135.

White, L. Implication of parametric variation for adult second language acquisition. *Language Learning*, 1986 (35), pp. 47-26.

White, L. Markedness and second language acquisition: The question of transfer. *Studies in Second Language Acquisition*, 1987b (9), pp. 261-286.

White, L. Second language acquisition: From initial to final state. In J. Archibald (ed.), *Second Language Acquisition and Linguistic Theory*. Oxford: Blackwell, 2000, pp. 30-155.

White, L. Fossilization in steady state L2 grammars: Implications of persistent problems with inflectional morphology. *Bilingualism: Language and Cognition*, 2003, 6(2), pp. 129-141.

Wierzbicka, A. *The Semantics of Grammar*. Amsterdam, John

Benjamins, 1988

Wong, E. and T. Quek. Acquisition of the English definite article by Chinese and Malay ESL learners. *Electronic Journal of Foreign Language Teaching*, 2007, 4(2), pp. 210-223.

Yang, M. and T. Ionin. L2 English articles and the computation of uniqueness. In J. Crawford et al. (eds.), *Proceedings of the 3rd Conference on Generative Approaches to Language Acquisition North America*. Somerville, MA: Cascadilla Proceedings Project, 2008, pp. 325-335.

Yavaş, M. Sonority and the acquisition of #sC clusters. *Journal of Multilingual Communication Disorders*, 2006, 4(3), pp. 159-168.

Yavaş, M. and J. Barlow. Acquisition of #sC clusters in Spanish-English bilingual children. *Journal of Multilingual Communication Disorders*, 2006, 4(3), pp. 182-193.

Young, R. Form-function relations in articles in English interlanguage. In R. Baylay and D. R. Preston (eds.), *Second Language Acquisition and Linguistic Variation*. Amsterdam: John Benjamins, 1996, pp. 133-175.

Yuh-Fang, Chang. How to say no: An analysis of cross-cultural difference and pragmatic transfer. *Language Sciences*, 2009, 31(4), pp. 477-493.

Žegarac, V. Relevance Theory and "the" in Second Language Acquisition. *Second Language Research*, 2004, 20(3), pp. 193-211.

Zhou, B. G. *The Use of English Articles by Chinese EFL Learners*. Nanjing: Nanjing University Press, 2006.

Zobl, H. The formal and developmental selectivity of L1 influence on L2 acquisition. *Language Learning*, 1980a (30), pp. 43-57.

Zobl, H. Developmental and transfer errors: Their common bases and (possibly) differential effects on subsequent learning. *TESOL Quarterly*, 1980b(14), pp. 469-479.

Zobl, H. A direction for Contrastive Analysis: The comparative study of developmental sequences. *TESOL Quarterly*, 1982 (16), pp. 169-183.

Zobl, H. Markedness and the projection problem. *Language Learning*, 1983(33), pp. 293-313.

Zobl, H. Cross-language generalizations and the contrastive dimension of the interlanguage hypothesis. In Davies et al. (eds.), *Interlanguage*. Edinburgh: Edinburgh University Press, 1984, pp. 79-97.

陈平:《释汉语中与名词性成分相关的四组概念》,《中国语文》1987年第2期。

戴炜栋、韦理:《中国学习者英语冠词语义特征习得研究》,《外语教学与研究》2008年第40卷第2期。

李景泉、蔡金亭:《中国英语写作中的冠词误用现象》,《解放军外国语学报》2001年第24卷第6期。

寮非:《第二语言习得中母语迁移现象分析》,《外语教学与研究》1998年第114卷第2期。

宁筘:《中国大学生英语冠词习得研究》,《中国英语教学》2009年第8期。

沈家煊:《不对称和标记理论》,江西教育出版社1999年版。

王剑:《中国学生英语定冠词非类指用法的习得》,《外语教学》2005年第26卷第3期。

韦理、戴炜栋:《大学生英语定冠词句法接口研究》,《中国外语》2010 年第 7 卷第 2 期。

闫莉莉:《中国英语冠词初探》,《外语教学与研究》2003 年第 35 卷第 3 期。

杨梅:《英语冠词二语习得研究:历史与现状》,《北京第二外国语学院学报》2009 年第 10 期。

周保国:《第二语言习得中英语定冠词过度使用研究》,《当代外语》2007 年第 30 卷第 4 期。

周保国:《英语冠词系统二语习得研究》,武汉大学出版社 2008 年版。

朱叶秋:《大学生英语冠词掌握情况调查》,《外语教学与研究》2003 年第 35 卷第 3 期。

朱永平:《第二语言习得难度的预测及教学策略》,《语言教学与研究》2004 年第 6 卷第 4 期。

Acknowledgements

In the process of writing this book, I have received valuable help and support at every stage of the work from a number of people without whom it is impossible for me to complete it. First and foremost, I am greatly indebted to my supervisor, Prof. Dai Weidong who is the right person to lead me to the field of second language acquisition and has instructed me in the theoretical study and given me kind help at every step of the research. His encouragement, patience, and the critical comments have always been the incentive to keep me going. I benefit a lot from his in-class courses and off-class discussion and talks from which I absorbed the original and creative ideas with respect to second language acquisition. It would be impossible for me to conduct the research and finish the book without his constant guidance and help.

I'm also very grateful to the professors in Shanghai International Studies University for their valuable knowledge and inspiration I have got from their lectures, especially to professor Luo Xuemei for her instruction of data analysis and how to use the software of SPSS.

I would further like to thank all the participants and the teachers in the University of Central Lancashire (UCLan) in the process of experiments. The participants tried their best to cooperate with me and to finish the experiments in time, which guarantees the validity of the experiments. Professor Michael Wood spared no effort to help me, asking the students to finish the tasks in class and collecting the data for me. I would also thank him for his help with the classification of articles and other determiners together with the analysis of types of reasons.

My special gratitude goes to Yang Liuyan who gave me many valuable suggestions and my friends who helped me to transcribe the interviews which needed much effort.

Finally, I want to express my thanks to the support and encouragement from my family members in the whole process of the book writing.